CULTURE
Trumps Everything

THE UNEXPECTED TRUTH
ABOUT THE WAYS ENVIRONMENT CHANGES
BIOLOGY, PSYCHOLOGY, AND BEHAVIOR

Gustavo R. Grodnitzky, Ph.D

ISBN: 978-0-9907279-0-3 (Paperback)
ISBN: 978-0-9907279-1-0 (Hardcover)

Library of Congress Control Number: 2014915794

Published by
MountainFrog Publishing

Website: www.DrGustavo.com

Cover Design: Heather Neil

Publisher's Cataloging-in-Publication Data:
Grodnitzky, Gustavo R.
    Culture trumps everything: the unexpected truth about the ways environment changes biology, psychology, and behavior / Gustavo R. Grodnitzky.
    pages cm
    Includes bibliographical references and index.
    ISBN: 978-0-9907279-0-3 (pbk.)
    ISBN: 978-0-9907279-1-0 (hardcover)
    ISBN: 978-0-9907279-2-7 (e-book)
    1. Culture—Economic aspects. 2. Economics—Sociological aspects. 3. Capitalism—Social aspects. 4. Success in business. I. Title.
HM548 .G76 2014
306.3`42—dc23

                                        2014915794

To my wife, Eve,
without whose *substantial* editing skills, this
book would not be complete.
You have provided a light when the world is
dark and shelter when it is stormy.
You have shown me a love I would otherwise have never known.

and

To my parents, who had the courage to leave the only
country and culture they had ever known, for the promise
of opportunity and the chance to raise their children in the
United States. This book is, in part, a result of that decision.

CONTENTS

PREFACE..vii

INTRODUCTION xi

CHAPTER 1 | CULTURE...1

CHAPTER 2 | BEHAVIORAL NORMS 27

CHAPTER 3 | CORPORATE MODELS......................................53

CHAPTER 4 | HABIT PATTERNS 79

CHAPTER 5 | CONNECTEDNESS...103

CHAPTER 6 | TRUST 125

CHAPTER 7 | LANGUAGE..157

CHAPTER 8 | TIME PERSPECTIVE..175

CHAPTER 9 | QUINTESSENCE AND CULTURE SHIFT.. 199

REFERENCES..225

ACKNOWLEDGMENTS..235

INDEX 237

ABOUT THE AUTHOR..243

PREFACE

I was standing in a prison cell that was about six feet wide by eight feet long. The cell had cinderblock walls, painted an institutional blue-gray, and a white cement floor. On the ceiling there was a long, narrow fluorescent light, the kind that makes people look half-dead. It was flush with the ceiling to prevent tampering, and so it could not be used as a beam to hang oneself with a bed sheet. In the cell there was also an industrial-strength sink bolted to the blue-gray wall with a steel mirror above it, a toilet that could be dropped from a four-story building and barely get a scratch, and a set of bunk beds made of gray steel, with a plastic-covered mattress, a single sheet and blanket, and a pillow that was thin enough to fit in an antique mail slot.

I was leaning against the sink. Across from me sat Tony, gazing into space, with a forlorn look on his face. Tony was a mafia *capo*, a "Family" member who ran a crew and was on trial for conspiracy and murder. Tony was feeling depressed because his wife had decided to leave him, and there was little he could do from inside prison.

All of a sudden I heard a "body alarm," which is a radio alarm that corrections officers activate when they are in danger or distress. I jumped up, ran out of the cell, and turned right, running toward the common area in the center of the unit, where I could hear the body alarm was activated. As I approached the end of the range, where the line of cells met the common area, I looked towards the central part of the unit and saw an enormous brawl. Inmates were swinging chairs like sledgehammers, flinging pool balls through the air like snowballs, and wielding pool cues as bats. I paused, just for a moment, and thought,

These are the times when inmates settle scores. This is when people die in prison.

The next thing I remember, I felt an arm coming over my right shoulder, across my neck and chest, and a hand grabbing my armpit on my left side. I felt the full weight of an adult male, well over 200 pounds, pulling me backwards and down to the floor. I had no idea who it was, but at that moment, there was little I could do other than put my hands behind me, bracing for what I anticipated would be a brutal impact. The impact never came.

Instead, I suddenly found myself surrounded by eight of Tony's foot soldiers: "wise guys," all of whom were made men. Both these terms signify they were officially inside the Family and had pledged their loyalty to the boss and the Family for life. All at once, these made men were holding me back, shielding me from flying debris, and keeping any other inmate who tried to approach me at bay. They were protecting me, doing everything they could to keep me from being harmed in any way.

Some of these "made men" were the same people who, several weeks earlier, had literally dangled a psychologist from the eleventh-floor window of a New York City office building, by his ankles, because they suspected he was the one who was empowering Tony's wife to leave him. Why would a group of mafia "made men" protect and shield me from harm? These men all had a history of murder, yet they were protecting me from getting as much as a scratch.

Perhaps if I had been part of Tony's crew, part of the "Family," it would have been expected and normal for them to protect me as they protected each other. But that wasn't the case here. I was an outsider, and they had protected me anyway. Even though I was not part of their culture, they behaved as if I were.

I know well that under different circumstances, in the course of day-to-day life on the street outside of prison, if I had been someone who was being uncooperative, or if I just didn't agree to whatever terms they were offering me, they would have done to me what they did to so many others. This could range from verbal threats, to physical intimidation, or even "clipping" (i.e., murder) if the need arose. But they did none of these things. On that day, they united to protect and defend me. Why?

This question occupied my thinking for months. At the time, I was working as a psychologist at the Metropolitan Correction Center – New York, (MCC-NY) in downtown Manhattan, and working closely with Tony. He was dangerously suicidal, and my role was to ensure he did not kill himself, by turning him away from his suicidal thinking. To his crew and "Family," I was the one environmental factor that was keeping Tony alive. In these circumstances, in that environment, murderers – literally – can and did behave in a way that was protective of human life. When the prison brawl broke out, I did not ask them to protect me; I did not teach them to protect me; I did not pay them to protect me – the circumstances and the environment demanded it of them.

What I finally came to understand is that I had fundamentally changed the environment for Tony and his crew. Specifically, I had changed four critical components of their environment:

- *Connectedness.* I had connected with Tony in a way that no one else outside the "Family" had done. He knew that I genuinely wanted to diminish his suffering. It was this connection that his crew believed was keeping him alive.
- *Trust.* I had earned their trust by always doing what I said I was going to do and showing genuine concern about Tony's despair.
- *Language.* I had learned their language so I could understand what they were trying to communicate in a succinct and meaningful way.
- *Time Perspective.* When I was in danger, they understood they needed to act in that moment or I would have been injured – or worse.

These four factors – connectedness, trust, language, and time perspective – are the seeds that were planted in a barren environment, yet took root enough to keep me from harm. Each is covered as an independent chapter in this book to illustrate how you might plant these same seeds in your organizational culture.

If murderers can become protective of human life in response to changed environmental circumstances, just imagine what is possible in our own lives, for our coworkers and employees, and for the world.

INTRODUCTION

I've always been curious. I'm fascinated by how things work. As a child, I remember following my grandfather around as he would fix things, adjust things, and make things with his hands in ways that I found profoundly fascinating. My grandfather was very much a "Mr. Fix-It," and I wanted to understand his approach to finding solutions. It was clear that his first step was finding out how things worked before doing what he could to fix, adjust, or change them. His impact on my desire to understand the world and how it worked cannot be overstated.

As a young child, I remember taking things apart and putting them back together to try to understand how they worked. OK, let's be honest, it was mostly me taking things apart and leaving them in pieces strewn about the floor; only occasionally would I put them back together. Toys, radios, cassette players, and boom boxes; if they were within my reach and had a visible opening, they were at my mercy.

Growing up in a house with a mother who was a clinical social worker and a father who was a psychiatrist, I became aware of many psychological concepts and constructs at an early age, one of them being the construct of personality. As with most people, I was taught that one's personality is "part of who you are" and that it is important to have a "good" personality. In my family of origin, as in society, a "good" personality meant having perceived qualities of extroversion: being outgoing, friendly, warm, and approachable.

Yet, there was something about the construct of a "good" personality that just didn't make sense to me. Something didn't "work." As a child and adolescent, wanting to please the adults around me, I tried to develop what others would call a "good" personality. Yet, there were times and situations that my behavior would be "outside" my personality. In certain situations, I could be quiet or withdrawn, yet engaged. In others I might be downright aloof and distant. These behaviors did not correlate with the personality I had developed, or for which I was known.

Furthermore, as I became a young adult, I began to make similar observations of others. Although most people had well-developed, identifiable personalities, they were also quite capable of behaving in ways well outside what their personalities would suggest or predict. I saw people who were normally well-intentioned and friendly behave in ways that were ruthless and brutal, and, conversely, I saw acts of great compassion from people whom you would least expect it of, as discussed in the preface of this book.

The prison incident described in the preface, where my life was literally saved by murderers, was a life-altering event. It changed my view of the world and human behavior, and it sent me on a journey to look at human behavior in a way that is different from many other people's perspectives. It is this journey (thus far) that has prompted the creation of this book.

I have designed this book to be actionable, and every chapter follows a consistent format. The first section of every chapter is titled *What You Need to Know*. This is a topline summary of the chapter, with each point being a possibly controversial and challenging truth. Each statement in *What You Need to Know* can also be found inside the chapter with the supporting evidence for the statement. Each chapter closes with a section called *So What?*, which is a narrative summary of the chapter, and a *Taking Action* section that includes several questions regarding how you can immediately take action and create change with the information that was presented in the chapter.

The prison incident helped me develop a real appreciation for the psychological law of predictive behavior. It states that the best predictor of future behavior is past behavior, *given the same circumstances.* Behavior doesn't occur in a vacuum. It occurs in the context of an environment with beliefs, behavioral rules, traditions, and rituals. It is these beliefs, behavioral rules, traditions, and rituals that make up a critical part of our environment that I refer to as culture. Although this book is focused specifically on organizational culture, I believe that as a reader, you will see that the concepts and constructs introduced here are also broadly applicable to culture writ large. It is the cultures we belong to, which in some circumstances we create and in others we simply find ourselves, that most successfully predict human behavior.

Each chapter in this book represents a critical component of culture. In the more than twenty years that I have been a psychologist (fifteen of those years as a consultant and professional speaker), I have seen people behave in a variety of ways that can be described as both inside or outside their personality. I have often heard people observe the behavior of others and say, "That doesn't make sense" or "That is so outside his or her personality." In these instances, I believe that people fail to take into account the power of culture and its influence on human behavior.

I wrote this book to try to help people look at human behavior through a different lens. Although we all remain responsible for our own behaviors in every circumstance, when we look at behavior in the context of culture, I believe that behavior becomes clearer. As adults, we all bear some responsibility for creating the environment and culture in which we live. I have learned both personally and professionally that culture is often an exacerbating or mitigating factor in human behavior. When we consider culture, even human behavior that would otherwise seem "crazy" becomes much more understandable.

This book has taken my education and twenty plus years of experience and organized it in a way that I hope will allow others to look at human behavior as the complex phenomenon that it is, understanding that *culture trumps everything.*

CHAPTER 1

CULTURE

"Culture is the widening of the mind and of the spirit."

– Jawaharlal Nehru,
First Prime Minister of India

What You Need To Know:

1. The Law of Predictive Behavior: The best predictor of future behavior is past behavior, given the same circumstance.

2. DNA is your hardware; epigenetics is your software.

3. Every cell in your body contains your entire DNA; your epigenetics is what tells your cells what to become and how to function.

4. Putting yourself in a toxic culture or environment, such as one with stress, poor food, or lack of activity, can shorten your life.

5. Epigenetics shows us that the culture we create for ourselves not only changes our biology, but also the biology of our children and grandchildren.

6. We mistakenly tend to make attributions of behaviors to individuals rather than their situations, circumstances, or culture.

7. When a policy and culture clash, and no one is present to enforce the policy, culture will win time and time again.

8. We too often focus on changing a policy rather than focusing on changing culture.

9. Policies tell people what NOT to do; culture tells people what TO do. Policies *limit* behavior. Culture *drives* behavior.

10. Look at culture first; it is a better predictor of behavior than biology or psychology.

Culture – which I define as the environment in which we live and work, including the beliefs, behavioral rules, traditions, and rituals that bind us together – is a better predictor of future behavior than biology or personality. When you are dealing with day-to-day events, critical circumstances, and in almost all other situations: *culture trumps everything*. This becomes clear when one considers the psychological Law of Predictive Behavior.

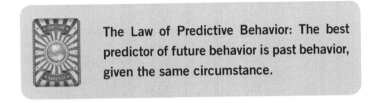

The Law of Predictive Behavior: The best predictor of future behavior is past behavior, given the same circumstance.

Psychology, unlike physics or chemistry, is considered a very new science. In contrast, physics, as a science, can trace its origins back to around the year 600 BCE and the Greek philosopher Thales, who is often referred to as "the father of science." Thales insisted that naturally occurring phenomena have explanations in the natural world, rather than in the divine. Modern chemistry can be traced back to Antoine-Laurent de Lavoisier, a French chemist who in 1789 established the law of Conservation of Mass, stating that the mass of a closed system must remain constant over time.

By contrast, psychology, the study of human behavior, has only really been a science for about fifty years, with the advent of behavioral and cognitive psychology. Being a new science, it has very few laws. One of its well-known but often misunderstood laws is the Law of Predictive Behavior: the best predictor of future behavior is past behavior, given the same circumstances.

This law has some nuance, which too often gets lost or misquoted, so stick with me. Saying that the best predictor of future behavior is past behavior, given the same circumstance, means that in order to understand and predict human behavior into the future, you must not only consider past behavior (individual characteristics, personality, and so on, which is where most people believe the statement/law ends) but also the circumstances, environment, or context of that behavior.

Behavior does not occur in a vacuum. It occurs in a context of interactions between individuals or groups with their surroundings. If you truly want to understand and predict what a person is going to do in the future, you must consider not only past behaviors but also the environment in which those behaviors took place.

We see law enforcement applying this psychological law every day. If you read about a bank robbery in your local newspaper, the police first go to the scene of the robbery to collect evidence. Then, invariably, who do the police go to interview and investigate first? People in the area who have been convicted of bank robbery. If there is a story about a fire that was attributed to arson, the police first go to the scene of the arson to collect evidence. Again, invariably, who do police go to interview and investigate first? People in the area who have been convicted of arson.

This is also precisely why, in business, when we are looking to hire a new employee, we ask for a resume or curriculum vitae (CV). Both serve as a history of past professional performance. The assumption is that, if candidates have demonstrated exceptional performance in other organizations in the past, they will also demonstrate exceptional performance for us in our organization in the future. Sadly, too often this turns out not to be the case. Why? Do all candidates lie on their resume? Do all references lie when you speak to them? The answer lies in the last clause of the Law of Predictive Behavior: *given the same circumstance*. When new hires join our organization, by definition they are entering a (often radically) different set of circumstances. The set of circumstances or the overall environment within an organization is what I refer to as corporate culture – and it is generally our corporate culture that ultimately dictates the performance of our employees, both new and existing.

Saying that culture trumps everything means that if employees within your organization are goal-oriented, team-focused, and driven by performance, it is because your culture demands it. Conversely, if your organization has employees that don't care about goals, don't care about teams, and don't care about performance, it is because your culture allows that, as well. It is important to understand that culture is very much like a garden. Left unattended, a garden will grow all sorts of weeds and plants that you have no interest in growing and that will actually choke out the fruits, the vegetables and the flowers you do want to grow. But, if you spend time in your garden – if you spend time on your culture – and you go through picking out the weeds and plants you don't want to grow, it becomes a lot easier to grow the fruits, the vegetables, and the flowers you *do* want to grow.

Spending time in the garden of your culture means that focusing on your organizational culture is the difference between working *on* your business vs. working *in* your business. Working *on* your business means working *on* your culture because culture trumps everything.

To understand how culture trumps everything, this chapter will look at two specific factors that heavily influence behavior – biology and psychology – and will illustrate how culture shapes (and ultimately trumps) both of these factors.

Culture Trumps Biology

Epigenetics is an exciting new field that has turned genetics on its head. It is the study of the ways that the *expression* of our genes is modified by environmental influences without actually changing our DNA. Epigenetics puts hard science behind what humans have long known, which is that when we optimize our environment and behavior, we move our minds and bodies to perform at higher levels. That is why epigenetics is part of the key to understanding how and why culture trumps our biology.

Scientists and people at large have long underestimated the potent effect of the environment on our biology. When Charles Darwin wrote *On the Origin of Species*[1] more than 150 years ago, the environment was seen as a critical factor in selecting traits that would be passed on to a species' offspring, ensuring the survival of that species. What Darwin, and others since, did *not* imagine was the short-term changes produced by the environment on our epigenetics and the expressions of specific genes. It is our epigenetic tags that decide which genes get expressed or not.

What was unimaginable 150 years ago has been found to be scientific fact in the last 10 years. Culture – the environment we create through our beliefs, behavioral rules, traditions and rituals, including what we eat and drink, how we sleep, how we manage stress, and the activities we choose – trumps biology.

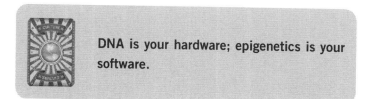

DNA is your hardware; epigenetics is your software.

To use a technology metaphor, think of your genome – your entire genetic information made up of DNA – as the hardware of a computer. Your epigenome is more like the software, which tells the hardware what to do. You can have Mac or PC, each with an Intel chip. The hardware (DNA/Intel chip) is the same. You can run Microsoft Windows products on a PC and Apple software on a Mac, both with an Intel chip. While both computers have the same hardware (DNA/Intel chip) the software will look and behave differently. Although it is the genome itself (Intel chip) that actually *does* all the work, it is the epigenome (software) that is going to tell it *what* to do and how it should appear.

Every cell in your body contains your entire DNA; your epigenetics is what tells your cells what to become and how to function.

Your DNA – your hardware – is going to be the same throughout your entire life. But your epigenetic tags – your software – will change throughout your lifetime, based on the choices you make and the environment you create or find yourself in. Your environment trumps biology.

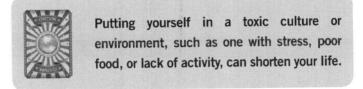

Putting yourself in a toxic culture or environment, such as one with stress, poor food, or lack of activity, can shorten your life.

The environment in which we work, including the beliefs and behavioral rules that bind us together in the workplace, is called corporate culture. This means that if you or your team wants to achieve exceptional performance, you don't have to look for a person who has exceptional genes or attributes; you just have to create an environment where they will behave in an exceptional way. Conversely, if you find yourself in an environment that is toxic (psychologically or biologically), not only will your performance suffer at work, but so will your biology. Toxic work environments can and do kill. In this way, culture trumps biology. Culture trumps everything.

How Norrbotten Changed the World

In the remote, snow-swept reaches of northern Sweden lies Norrbotten. It is north of the Arctic Circle, where there is an average of only six people per square mile. Within this tiny population, science began to reveal how genes can be influenced by the environments of everyday life.

Norrbotten has always been isolated; so much so that in the 19th century, if the area had a bad harvest, people starved to death. Yet other years the land gave with such abundance that the same people who had gone hungry in previous winters were able to gorge themselves for months. And of course they did. After being without food for months, how could you not? What made life more difficult still was that the years of starvation and abundance were completely unpredictable.

 Epigenetics shows us that the culture we create for ourselves not only changes our biology, but also the biology of our children and grandchildren.

In the 1980s, Dr. Lars Olov Bygren, a preventive-health specialist who is now at the prestigious Karolinska Institute in Stockholm, began to wonder what the long-term effects of feast and famine years on children growing up in Norrbotten in the 19th century might be — and not just on them, but on their children and grandchildren as well. So he drew a random sample of 99 individuals born in the Overkalix parish of Norrbotten in 1905 and used historical records to trace their parents and grandparents back to birth. By analyzing meticulous agricultural records, Bygren and two colleagues determined how much food had been available to these parents and grandparents when they were young.

The historical documents show that 1800, 1812, 1821, 1836, and 1856 were years of total crop failure, extreme suffering, starvation, and subsequent death. But in 1801, 1822, 1828, 1844, and 1863, the land produced and fed the community with such abundance that the same people who had gone hungry in previous winters were able to have their fill for months.

Around the time he started collecting the data, Bygren had become fascinated with research showing that conditions in the womb could affect your health not only when you were a fetus, but well into adulthood. In 1986, for example, *The Lancet* published the first of two groundbreaking papers[2,3] showing that if a pregnant woman ate poorly, her child would be at significantly higher than average risk for cardiovascular disease as an adult. Bygren wondered whether that effect could start even before pregnancy: could parents' experiences early in their lives somehow change the traits they passed to their offspring?

In the world of genetics, this idea was akin to sacrilege. From time immemorial, geneticists have had a certain understanding in biology: whatever choices people make during their lives might ruin their short-term memory, or make them fat, or hasten death, but these choices won't change their genes — their actual DNA. This was a fundamental belief in the world of genetics that meant that when we had kids of our own, the genetic slate would be wiped clean.

Moreover, any such effects of environment (nurture) on a species' genes (nature) can't happen quickly. Darwin espoused that evolutionary changes take place over many generations and through millions of years of natural selection. But Bygren and other scientists have now amassed historical evidence suggesting that environmental conditions can leave markers on the genetic material in eggs and sperm. These genetic markers can short-circuit evolution and not only change genetic expression within a generation, but also pass along new traits to the next generation. This means how you live your life today (for good or for ill) can affect not only your unborn children, but also your grandchildren.

In the first paper Bygren wrote about Norrbotten, which was published in 2001 in the Dutch journal *Acta Biotheoretica*,[4] Bygren's research showed that in Overkalix:

- Boys who enjoyed the town's rare overabundant winters actually had *shorter* lifespans.
- The sons and grandsons of the boys who went from normal eating to gluttony in a single season also lived far shorter lives.
- Sons and grandsons of Overkalix boys who had overeaten died an average of six years earlier.
- After controlling for socioeconomic variation, sons and grandsons whose forefathers did *not* experience starvation-to-gluttony within a single year lived an astonishing 32 years longer.

The original study just looked at male heredity. What about the girls? Later papers using different Norrbotten cohorts also found significant drops in lifespan and discovered that similar results were seen along the female line as well, meaning that the daughters and granddaughters of girls who had gone from normal to gluttonous diets also lived shorter lives.

To put it simply, Bygren's data showed that a single winter of overeating as a youngster could initiate a biological chain of events that would lead one's grandchildren to die decades earlier than their peers did.

The culture we create for ourselves, our colleagues, and coworkers not only changes our performance, it changes our biology. Culture trumps biology – and it does so through a mechanism known as epigenetics.

The Mechanics of Epigenetics

You have billions of cells in your body. Each cell contains the same exact genetic code. This is the blueprint for your body. Just because each cell has your entire DNA doesn't mean each cell knows how to use it. Cells need instructions. Epigenetics (literally meaning "above genetics") are the instructions that come from carbon and hydrogen compounds called methyl groups and proteins called histones.

The National Human Genome Research Institute (part of the National Institutes of Health) explains the functioning of the epigenome as follows:

> "The epigenome is made up of chemical compounds, some of which come from natural sources like food and others from man-made sources like medicines or pesticides. As it marks the genome with these chemical tags, the epigenome serves as the intersection between the genome and the environment.
>
> The epigenome marks your genome in two main ways, both of which play a role in [how genes are expressed – or not expressed].
>
> The first type of mark, called DNA methylation, directly affects the DNA in your genome. In this process, chemical tags called methyl groups attach to the backbone of the DNA molecule in specific places. The methyl groups

turn genes off or on by affecting interactions between DNA and the cell's protein-making machinery.

The second kind of mark, called histone modification, indirectly affects the DNA in your genome. Histones are spool-like proteins that enable DNA's very long molecules to be wound up neatly into chromosomes inside the cell nucleus. A variety of chemical tags can grab hold of the tails of histones, changing how tightly or loosely they package DNA. If the wrapping is tight, a gene may be hidden from the cell's protein-making machinery, and consequently be ['dialed down']. In contrast, if the wrapping is loosened, a gene that was formerly hidden may be ['dialed up'].["5]

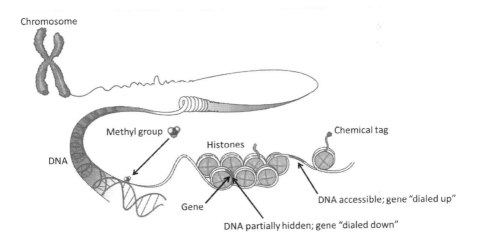

Figure 1: Impact of methyl groups and histones on epigenetics.

To use an analogy, methyl groups are more like an on/off switch for your genes, whereas histones are more like a dimmer switch or volume dial. Every cell in your body has what is referred to as a specific methylation and histone pattern. These are what give every cell its own unique orders for expression. This is precisely what makes a skin cell, a skin cell; an eye cell, an eye cell; a heart cell, a heart cell; a kidney cell, a kidney cell.

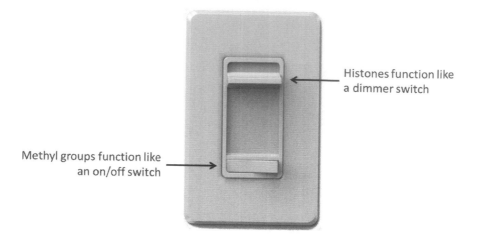

Figure 2. Analogy of methyl group functioning like a light switch and histone functioning like a dimmer switch.

This is also why stem cells are so powerful and so promising to our medical future. Stem cells can become any cell in the body because they do not yet have a specific methylation and histone pattern. Based on the tissue environment where they are placed, stem cells can "pick up" the methylation and histone pattern of the cells around them, becoming any cell they need to be. In this way, on a cellular level, our cells respond to the environment in which they are placed.

Another way of thinking about genetics and epigenetics is to look at how we understand a sentence. Your genes, or your DNA, are like the letters and spaces that make up the words in a sentence. Your epigenetics are the punctuation in the sentence. In combination, they determine the meaning of the sentence.

For example, if your genome (DNA) were a series of letters and spaces that make up words, it might look like this (intentionally without punctuation):

"I love food like most people one of my favorites is pepperoni pizza Grandpa introduced me to Hawaiian style a few weeks ago and I didn't think I'd like it but I'll try anything once let's eat Grandpa"

Different patterns of punctuation (epigenetics) in the above sentence would lead to drastically different interpretations (expression), even when the letters and words are in precisely the same order.

Example 1: "I love food like most people. One of my favorites is pepperoni pizza. Grandpa introduced me to Hawaiian style a few weeks ago, and I didn't think I'd like it. But I'll try anything once. Let's eat, Grandpa!"

Example 2: "I love food. Like most people, one of my favorites is pepperoni pizza. Grandpa introduced me to Hawaiian style a few weeks ago. And I didn't think I'd like it but I'll try anything – once! Let's eat Grandpa!"

Even with the letters and words in exactly the same order, the changes in punctuation make the meaning of these sentences completely different. In case one, you are inviting your grandfather to eat pizza. In case two, you are suggesting cannibalism!

Changes in Your Epigenome

Epigenetic information is not permanent. It can change over time throughout your life, particularly when your body is going through a lot of changes, such as during puberty or pregnancy. But it's not only during these radical changes in our lives that we see changes to our epigenome. Environmental factors – such as what we do, what we eat, whether we smoke, and how we manage stress – also make a big difference.

Science has known about the epigenome since the 1970s, but it's only since the late 1990s that scientists have understood the effect these epigenetic "tags" can have on our DNA. For example, a bad diet can lead to methyl groups binding to the wrong place and making mistakes. With these incorrect instructions, cells become abnormal and can become a disease, such as cancer or an autoimmune disease.

The food we take into our bodies changes our epigenetics. The Bygren studies show us that these changes not only affect us, but can also affect our children and grandchildren. However, Bygren's work was not able to specifically identify the mechanisms by which these epigenetic changes occurred. Fortunately, recent advances in biological science allow us to more directly understand the specific mechanisms at work.

Metabolic Derangement

Statistically, the U.S. has an overweight and obesity rate that hovers around 69%.[6] At the same time, its cultural mores place great emphasis on being thin. This cultural script frequently drives behavior for people to consume low-fat, low-sugar, diet drinks, which generally contain artificial sweeteners. When we consume drinks with artificial sweeteners, it can change our biology.

In September of 2013, Susan Swithers, a professor of behavioral neuroscience at Purdue University, published an article in the journal, *Trends in Endocrinology and Metabolism*.[7] It was a review of the past twenty years of research on commonly used artificial sweeteners, including sucralose, aspartame, saccharin, and others. Part of the findings discuss a concept of "metabolic derangement," meaning how the body can actually get confused by ingesting artificial sweeteners, leading to various problems such as risk of:

- Weight gain and obesity
- Type 2 diabetes
- Heart disease
- Stroke
- Metabolic syndrome: high blood pressure, high blood sugar, high triglycerides, low HDL (good) cholesterol levels, and excess belly fat – all of which increase the risk of heart disease and diabetes.

The "must be thin" culture in the United States drives many people to consume beverages that are low-calorie and contain artificial sweeteners. These drinks become part of the environment that feeds our cells throughout our bodies. These artificial sweeteners not only have a paradoxical effect on weight and health, but can also change our biology.

Consider the world before artificial sweeteners: when the body consumed something sweet, such as a fruit or a piece of candy (both containing sugar), as soon as the sweet taste hit the mouth, the brain anticipated the arrival of calories and sugar. As a result of this anticipation, the body produced physiological and metabolic changes, activating hormones such as GLP1 and insulin to assist in the regulation of blood sugar and satiation – all of which ultimately also provided a cardio-protective effect.

Now think about what happens when we begin to introduce artificial sweeteners into our system. We get a strong sweet taste in our mouth, and our bodies prepare for additional calories and sugars … but they never come. Over time, the body adjusts to this new environment, decreasing or eliminating the release of these sugar-processing, cardio-protective hormones (GLP1 and insulin). This is an evolutionary mechanism executed by the body simply to conserve energy and resources. If the body detects that it does not need to produce a specific hormone, it will stop producing it and conserve the energy it takes to produce that hormone.

Epigenetic science suggests that it is these precise types of changes that occur on an epigenetic level. You have the genes that instruct cells to produce these cardio-protective and sugar-processing hormones (GLP1 and insulin), but the environment (the artificial sweeteners you consume) creates a change in your epigenetics that reduces or shuts down the genes that are responsible for creating them. So, over time and with repetition, when people who regularly consume artificial sweeteners then bite into a piece of fruit, apple pie, or chocolate cake – all of which have real sugar – their bodies are no longer prepared to process the real sugars and calories. Dr. Swithers suggests this leads to diseases such as obesity, Type 2 diabetes, heart disease, stroke, and metabolic syndrome.

In her review, Swithers found studies that showed differences in metabolic function between people who drank no diet soda and people who drank as few as three cans of diet soda per week. Science still can't predict precisely who will or won't be adversely affected by the consumption of artificial sweeteners, but it is showing that its consumption does indeed change our prospects for good health.

This is just one example of how the environment we create – in this case, the food that we ingest, which is so often driven by culture – can and does change our biology. Similarly, the environments we create in our homes and places of work, which are also driven by culture, can shape our biology.

Genetic Blueprint

Until recently, it was thought that genes were the be-all and end-all of what you could be. They were your blueprint, and you couldn't escape them. This led to a particular social prejudice. Looking at the data without considering social and epigenetic factors, one could (incorrectly) conclude that people who are lower on the socioeconomic scale have less intelligence. In fact, as recently as the year 2000, there were scientists who still believed some people just have better genes for intelligence than others. Many still believe that poor people are poor because they have poor genes for intelligence. However, this couldn't be further from the truth. Not only are there a huge number of social factors that affect how well people will perform on an intelligence test, but a genetic trait is not just a function of genes (genetics), it's also a product of how the environment affects those genes (epigenetics).

In a series of articles published during the first week of December 2013, it was revealed that in 1953, a midwife at a Tokyo hospital accidentally switched two babies after their baths. One had been born to wealthy parents and was switched with one born to impoverished parents. The baby born to impoverished parents – but who grew up in the wealthy family – went to college and went on to run a successful real estate company. By contrast, the baby who was born to wealthy parents – but who grew up in an impoverished family – did not graduate high school, drives a delivery truck, and lives in a cramped one-room apartment.

Clearly, what was previously considered the "poor genes" or "wealthy genes" they were born with was trumped by the environment in which they were raised.

In a recent study from the University of South Florida's Department of Integrative Biology,[8] scientists Aaron Schrey and Courtney Coon state, "If you have two individuals with the same DNA sequence, you can get differences in their traits just by regulating what portions of the DNA sequence are turned on and off. When you expand this up to the population level, you begin to appreciate how fast variation can arise from environmental changes."

Culture Trumps Psychology

There is a widely held belief that people have a tendency to behave in a consistent way based on their particular personality style or profile. "Eve is shy." "Mark is lazy." "Karen is bossy." Saying that culture trumps personality means that although personality is a tendency to behave in a particular way, the environment or culture in which we find ourselves has a more significant influence on our behavior than we realize.

We see this organizational focus on individual characteristics or traits most clearly in hiring practices. According to the National Association of Colleges and Employers Job Outlook survey (2013),[9] the top ten characteristics employers want in their employees are:

1. Communication skills (verbal and written)
2. Honesty/integrity
3. Teamwork skills (works well with others)
4. Strong work ethic
5. Analytical skills

6. Flexibility/adaptability
7. Interpersonal skills (relates well to others)
8. Motivation/initiative
9. Computer skills
10. Detail-oriented

A full 50% of the characteristics desired by the National Association of Colleges and Employers Job Outlook survey are indeed personality traits. This is because of the long-held belief that certain personality traits must offer us some guarantee about certain levels of performance.

The top five personality traits employers want according to *Forbes Magazine*[10] are:

1. Professionalism (86%)
2. High energy (78%)
3. Confidence (61%)
4. Self-monitoring (58%)
5. Intellectual curiosity (57%)

These are the top characteristics and/or personality traits that employers are looking for in their employees. These are the characteristics that, theoretically, are supposed to be the best predictors of performance in our organizations. This is the judgment of most recruiters and recruiting professionals.

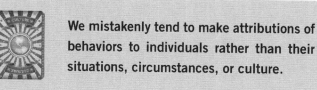

We mistakenly tend to make attributions of behaviors to individuals rather than their situations, circumstances, or culture.

This illustrates the fundamental attribution error explained by misattribution theory, which is that we tend to make attributions of behaviors to individual traits rather than to situations. We do this for two reasons: (1) our society emphasizes individual accomplishments, and (2) we have difficulty admitting how easily we can be influenced by situational forces. But, as we know, culture trumps everything.

At some level, we know this intuitively. If you take someone who is loud and boisterous and always speaking at the top of their lungs, and you walk that person into a museum, a church, or a bank – what are they likely to do? They're going to get quiet. Have you changed any of their personal attributes, skills, or personality? No. What have you changed? Their environment – you changed their environment, and the behavior follows. As we defined earlier, in your organizations, culture is the environment in which we live and work, including the beliefs, behavioral rules, traditions, and rituals that bind us together. When you change your employees' and coworkers' corporate culture, their behavior follows.

We can see this illustrated in the following examples, all of which feature individuals who were selected specifically for personality characteristics such as integrity, good judgment, and intelligence. However, in each example, those personality characteristics for which they were chosen were trumped by the environment and the culture in which these individuals found themselves, invariably with dire consequences for them and those around them.

Secret Service Psychology

Like many law enforcement agencies, the Secret Service recruits members by looking at the three basic personality characteristics believed to predict success in a law enforcement career. I will refer to them as the ABCs of law enforcement:

- A: Average to above average intelligence to facilitate and support good judgment.
- B: Behavior within normal limits, which is legal and lacking in psychopathology.
- C: Conscientiousness, which is the ability to recognize and do what is right – and to do it well and thoroughly.

These are the fundamental personality characteristics sought for all law enforcement personnel. In the Secret Service, these characteristics are considered not only part of the core essentials, but also part of the culture, writ large.

Advance Team Goes Off the Rails

In April, 2012, President Barack Obama was preparing to go to Cartagena, Colombia, for the Summit of the Americas. As is commonplace before the arrival of the American president, the Secret Service sent an advance team to ensure that the venues the president would attend and the avenues of transport he would take would be safe.

However, it was the "extracurricular" activities of twelve of these agents that caused a national stir and quickly became known as the biggest scandal in Secret Service history. These agents went to a bar, got stinking drunk, bragged about working for President Obama, brought prostitutes back to their hotel, and refused to pay them. It was their refusal to pay them that ultimately led to their undoing.

Prostitution, as it turns out, is legal in Colombia. The only reason we heard about the scandal was that one of the prostitutes complained about her lack of payment to the hotel manager, who reported it to the local police, who reported it to the U.S. State Department.

How does a group of twelve elite law enforcement officers who are hired for personality traits such as good judgment, legal behavior, and conscientiousness find itself in such a situation? Because culture trumps psychology.

Were these twelve agents responsible for their own individual behavior in this situation?

Absolutely.

Did the culture of the advance team influence the agents' behavior?

Absolutely.

Culture vs. Policy

I am not suggesting that these twelve men were not responsible for their behavior. They absolutely were. I am not going to suggest that they should not have received appropriate consequences for their behavior. They did. All were either fired or forced to resign. What I am suggesting is that when put in the context of culture, their behavior can be seen as a sign or symptom of a larger problem.

If this had been the behavior of one rogue officer, that officer might have been disciplined and we might never have heard of the incident. However, this was not a single officer, but a dozen who took part in these behaviors as a group, which suggests that these were acceptable behaviors in their culture.

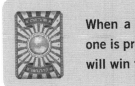

When a policy and culture clash, and no one is present to enforce the policy, culture will win time and time again.

For the Secret Service agents that travel as part of an advance team, this was clearly not an anomaly. Something this far outside the agency's behavioral norms does not occur all at once with a large group. It occurs incrementally over time in an environment that rewards – or simply fails to discourage – the behavior.

Furthermore, it is interesting to note that after the incident was first reported, the two supervisors for these officers briefly tried to cover up everyone's involvement, including their own. This is interesting because it suggests that these officers knew that what had been done was wrong. Although the official rules and the policies of the agency clearly made their behavior unacceptable, the culture made it acceptable … until they were caught.

Different Culture = Different Behavior

If the culture of the advance team had been closely yoked to the policies of the agency, one could imagine a situation where if one or two agents made a suggestion to go drinking and pick up women, then their peers, driven by culture, would have intervened and prevented that type of excursion. In this scenario, such aberrant behavior would not have been supported by the culture.

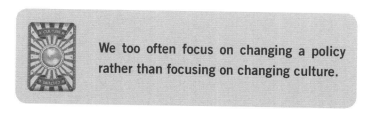

We too often focus on changing a policy rather than focusing on changing culture.

Sadly, the agency's response to a culture problem was to add more "common sense" rules and "refine" other rules, as if these twelve agents didn't already know or understand the existing rules and policies. In the future, agents deployed on foreign assignments will now receive briefings upon their arrival that include off-limit zones and establishments. Drinking alcohol within 10 hours of being on duty is now banned. Foreign nationals in hotel rooms, with the exception of hotel staff and official counterparts, will also now be banned. At other times, only moderate alcohol consumption will be permitted.

Policies tell people what NOT to do; culture tells people what TO do. Policies *limit* behavior. Culture *drives* behavior.

When highly trained, highly seasoned, elite law enforcement officers fail to follow rules, it is not because they don't know the rules. It is not necessarily because they have a problem with their character or personality. It is because the culture of the agency and/or situation in which they find themselves has greater influence over their behavior than does their character or personality. *Culture trumps psychology.*

In any organization, if a mistake is made because a rule or policy does not exist, it may make sense to create an appropriate one. However, if the rules and policies *are* in place and behavior *still* runs afoul of those rules or policies, leaders must consider culture as the culprit. Adding more rules doesn't change culture; changing behavioral norms changes culture.

Unfortunately, the Secret Service did not fully recognize the influence of culture on their agents' behavior, as evidenced by the fact that their "fix" was to add more rules rather than address cultural norms on the ground. By contrast, the response to an incident at Minot Air Force Base in North Dakota demonstrates a fuller understanding of how culture influences behavior.

Shaping Culture

In May of 2013, an Air Force Commander stripped seventeen of his senior officers of their authority to control and launch nuclear missiles and sent them to 60 to 90 days of training on how to do their jobs.

These officers were responsible for running the launch control centers for the Minuteman III nuclear missiles from Minot Air Force Base in North Dakota. Nuclear launch codes are not given to just anyone. They are only given to the most trusted senior officers, as they are responsible for the protocol that could initiate or respond to a nuclear attack.

These officers were well-versed in the rules and regulations of the Air Force and their positions. So what happened that would require this type of discipline and remediation?

The action was initiated by Lt. Col. Jay Folds, Deputy Commander for Minot Air Force Base in North Dakota. In a highly charged email, Folds began, "Did you know that we, as an operations group, have fallen – and it's time to stand ourselves back up?"

He continued, "We're discovering rot in the crew force," referring to the fact that he had learned that while on alert status, standing watch over the nuclear force, the unit was in violation of weapons safety rules and had compromised launch codes – and that others who had observed these violations had failed to report their behavior.

Folds' email later went on to clarify the situation by stating, "We are, in fact, in crisis now … we must crush any rules violators …." With this, Folds acknowledged that the problem was not the rules that were or were not in place. The problem was that the unit had developed a culture of complacency. They had developed a culture where the rules didn't matter as much, and they didn't need to be followed as closely.

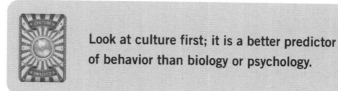

Look at culture first; it is a better predictor of behavior than biology or psychology.

Unlike the previous Secret Service example, Folds understood the behavior was an issue of culture. He went on to give very specific behavioral instructions to his unit that he believed would eliminate the complacency he had to deal with. This ranged from specific behavioral changes about enforcement of weapons safety rules and protection of launch codes all the way down to seemingly insignificant things such as "Clean your patches, uniforms, and get your hair cut." Folds understood that, when dealing with nuclear weapons, complacency is a slippery slope. He understood that to change a culture, what is needed is not more policies, but a greater adherence to agreed-upon behavioral norms: ensuring that people walk the walk.

So What?

As leaders, one of our primary concerns is ensuring the outstanding performance of our employees. To ensure this type of performance we must consider three things:

1. *Skill*: Does the person have the skill set to accomplish the task before them?
2. *Will*: Does the person have the desire to accomplish the task before them?
3. *Hill*: Are there organizational or cultural obstacles that will prevent them from accomplishing the task before them?

Generally, organizations overvalue the first two and discount the third. We hire people based on personality traits. We promote people based on technical competence. We train people based on individual skill gaps. All these circumstances focus on individual issues of skill and will.

But culture trumps biology. Culture trumps psychology. Culture trumps everything.

What we need to do is focus our efforts on creating a culture that supports the behaviors and performance we seek from our employees. As you will see in the chapters that follow, creating an environment using the desired behavioral norms that emphasizes connectedness, trust, shared language, and appropriate time perspective is crucial to an organization's success.

Taking Action

What can we do to ensure that our culture fosters the behaviors that advance the cause of the organization and eliminates those that work against it? Consider the following questions:

1. *Strengths*: What are the parts of your organization's culture that support high performance from your employees?
2. *Challenges*: What are the parts of your organization's culture that interfere with the high performance of your employees?
3. *Solutions*: What is one step you can take in the next 30 days to begin to overcome the challenges in your organization's culture?

CHAPTER 2

BEHAVIORAL NORMS

"People are going to behave however the social norms permit."

– Max Cannon,
Author and Cartoonist

What You Need to Know:

1. We live in two worlds: one of social norms and another of business norms. When business norms and social norms collide, social norms get pushed out.

2. When business norms are applied where or when social norms are in order, outcomes tend to be poor.

3. People work harder for cause than for cash. Purpose supersedes pay.

4. We must pay our employees fairly, competitively, and at a level that allows them to live a particular lifestyle.

5. Social norms create collaborative environments most would not anticipate. Business norms drive the type of competitiveness that can actually diminish collaboration.

6. Corporate loyalty does not have to be an oxymoron. Corporate loyalty is a social norm.

7. There are huge advantages to using social norms with customers and employees.

8. Social norms define a critical part of the culture we cultivate. They are the soil in which we plant the seeds of our organizational culture.

9. Money is the most expensive way to motivate people, and it does so only in the short term. Social norms are not only cheaper, but they last longer and are more effective.

10. Social norms deliver discretionary effort, flexibility, concern, and willingness to go the extra mile.

Behavioral Norms: Society's Rules of Engagement

Behavioral norms are the cultural rules of behavior that bind us together. They are the rules, implicit and explicit, that govern our behavior in society. Certain behavioral norms – such as "Thou shalt not kill" – are nearly universal, being found within almost all geographic, ethnic and religious groups. Other behavioral norms may be consistent within certain cultures, but vary widely between cultures. Direct eye contact, for example, is seen as a sign of honesty, confidence, and respect in the United States – but in Japan and China, it is generally considered disrespectful to make direct eye contact with someone who is your "superior."

Behavioral norms also exist in our social and work environments. What is most important to keep in mind is that behavioral norms are different and distinct from organizational policies. Policies tend to *limit* behavior (i.e. dress codes, travel restrictions, non-discrimination rules), whereas behavioral norms *drive and require* behavior (i.e. shaking hands when greeting, standing when making a presentation to a large group, and taking a genuine interest in coworkers).

Behavioral norms are the fertile ground in which we plant the seeds of organizational culture. In subsequent chapters, I will identify and discuss the behaviors that serve as the seeds of organizational culture to be planted within the fertile ground of behavioral norms. However, before I discuss the seeds to be planted, it is important to understand that we must prepare the soil through the selection of the appropriate behavioral norms. There are several types of behavioral norms; the most critical in a business environment are social norms and business norms.

Social Norms vs. Business Norms

We live in two worlds: one of social norms and another of business norms. Traditionally, business norms are used in business, and social norms are used in social settings. When business norms and social norms collide, social norms get pushed out. This is because business norms tend to be more precise than social norms, and particularly in business settings, people prefer clarity and have difficulty tolerating ambiguity.

> We live in two worlds: one of social norms and another of business norms. When business norms and social norms collide, social norms get pushed out.

Business norms typically have sharper edges. You get what you pay for, *quid pro quo*, and value is always tallied in the local currency. Prompt payment for services or products is expected, if not demanded. It is a world of comparable benefits. Business norms are the behavioral norms most often associated with CEOs and organizations that care about profitability – and little else. They believe that the bottom line is the be-all and end-all in business. This belief is also often associated with both a competitive need to win at all costs and a fear of being taken advantage of, which leads to a culture where people compete rather than collaborate, are compliant rather than creative (avoiding risk), and watch out for themselves rather than for their team or the organization as a whole.

Social norms are part of the world that includes friendly requests, social favors, and genuine interest and caring. For example, opening doors for others, giving up your seat on public transportation for an elderly person, and allowing others to go before you when merging into traffic (believe it or not, this does happen in certain parts of the country). In the world of social norms, instant payback is neither required nor expected. This creates less clarity and greater ambiguity that is more naturally accepted within the realm of social norms.

In reality, we inhabit both worlds simultaneously. Unfortunately, these are two worlds that don't mix well, and when they collide, difficulties arise. When business norms are applied where or when social norms are in order, outcomes tend to be poor.

For example, focusing on money (a business norm) makes us behave in ways economists anticipate, rather than as the social beings we naturally are. If people start doing something because they want to (for example, a cause or purpose) and you start paying them for it, the social norm is diminished. If a person's financial needs are not being met and you begin to pay that person for a product or service that they were previously giving away, they will focus on the business norm rather than the social norm.

Business Norms: When to Use Them

Business norms are most effectively used in transactional exchanges. When you walk into a store and want to buy a pack of gum, that gum has a specific value, as identified by its price. If you find the price acceptable, you exchange the equal value in the local currency for that pack of gum. In this case, both parties are perfectly satisfied with the exchange and transaction; there is nothing implied or expected regarding future behavior.

Business norms have a long history that focuses on transactions using money as a proxy for goods and services. In ancient times, money made trading easier. It saved you from carrying a side of beef to the market and deciding what portion of it was equivalent to four tomatoes. In modern times, money has provided even more benefits, from borrowing, to saving, to developing wealth, to creating transactional exchanges between people and businesses. Today, money has developed a life of its own. It has the capacity to diminish or remove the best in human interactions. We see this most clearly when business norms are applied in social settings.

I have a friend – we'll call him Fred. He is a very successful business executive who has made a lot of money. As a businessman, he tends to define and express his experiences, both business and social, in terms of financial metrics. His balance sheet is his Bible, and he has a tendency to know where he and it stand financially at any given moment.

 When business norms are applied where or when social norms are in order, outcomes tend to be poor.

Fred is divorced and just getting back into the dating world. He recently told me about a woman he was dating: smart, attractive, and successful. Of course, given his perspective, when he spoke about her, he couldn't leave out her job, how much money she made, and what he suspected was her net worth.

He had taken her out for dinner a few times for some very expensive cuisine. After the fourth dinner, on their way back to the car, Fred did a quick tally in his head and let her know how much of his hard-earned cash he had spent on the four dinners. I'll give you one guess as to what happened next.

Yes, not surprisingly, she refused to accept a ride home with him, called a cab, and never spoke to him again.

Something that might be closer to home for you: imagine you've been going to your in-laws' house for a traditional holiday dinner for years. One year, at your in-laws', at the end of the dinner, you say to your mother-in-law: "You have really outdone yourself this year. That was probably one of the best holiday dinners I've ever had. Really fantastic! Thanks so much …. What do I owe you? Is $100 enough? Maybe $150? How about $200?"

How might your mother-in-law respond? How about your spouse? Again, one guess is all it takes.

Business norms really can't be successfully applied in social settings, but might it be possible to apply social norms in a business setting? Might there be benefits to doing so?

The Power of Social Norms in Business Settings

It is clear that business norms in a social setting do not work effectively. In contrast, in what may be a surprise to many, social norms in a business setting generally work better than business norms.

The business case for applying social norms in a business setting has three parts. The first is that social norms improve employee performance. The second is that they facilitate collaboration. Finally, the third advantage of applying social norms in a business environment is the increase in corporate loyalty, which is a benefit that can only be achieved through social norms.

Performance

James Heyman of the University of California, Berkley, and Dan Ariely of the Massachusetts Institute of Technology, have done multiple experiments that demonstrate the power of social norms. In one experiment,[1] subjects were asked to sit in front of a computer screen and use a mouse to move a circle inside a square. This task was easy, boring, and repetitive. The subjects for the experiment were randomly assigned to four groups, each doing the task for a different incentive:

Group 1: Was paid $5 up front to do the task as many times as possible (business norm)

Group 2: Was paid $.50 for each circle (business norm)

Group 3: Was paid $.10 for each circle (business norm)

Group 4: Was asked to perform the task as a favor (social request, social norm)

What were the results?

Group 1:   Moved 159 circles
Group 2:   Moved 101 circles
Group 3:   Moved 100 circles
Group 4:   Moved 168 circles

These results have been repeated countless times since the experiment was first done. All results point to the same conclusion: subjects worked harder and performed better when applying social norms because *people work harder for cause than for cash. Purpose supersedes pay.* This requires us to connect and act based on human connectedness and belonging rather than money.

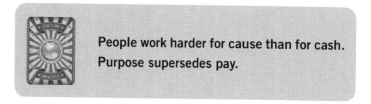

**People work harder for cause than for cash.
Purpose supersedes pay.**

We must pay our employees fairly, competitively, and at a level that allows them to live a particular lifestyle. This "takes money off the table."

It is important to note that those who were in Group 1, who were paid a flat fee, performed better than those who were paid per circle moved. In order to motivate using cause or purpose, we must take money off the table. The only way to do this is to pay people fairly, competitively, and at a level that allows them to achieve a certain level of relative comfort in their lives.

Leveraging social norms against business norms will often produce a more desirable outcome, not just in terms of employee performance, but also in terms of successful collaboration.

Collaboration

In most environments, lack of collaboration leads to failure, and collaboration leads to success. Especially in a knowledge economy, where growth relies on the quantity, quality, and accessibility of the information available (rather than on the means of production), social norms create collaborative environments most would not anticipate. Business norms drive the type of competitiveness that can actually diminish collaboration.

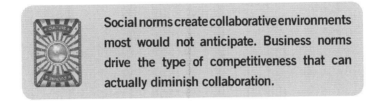

Social norms create collaborative environments most would not anticipate. Business norms drive the type of competitiveness that can actually diminish collaboration.

In another cognitive experiment, Kathleen Vohs of the University of Minnesota, Nicole Meade of Florida State University, and Miranda Goode of the University of British Columbia, asked participants to complete a scrambled word task, taking a set of scrambled words and making them into a sentence or phrase.[2]

Group 1: Received words that were considered neutral sentences (for example, "It's cold outside").

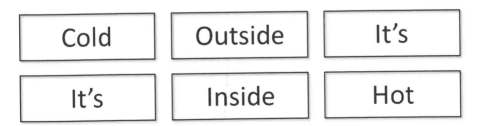

Group 2: Received words or phrases related to money (for example, "High-paying salary").

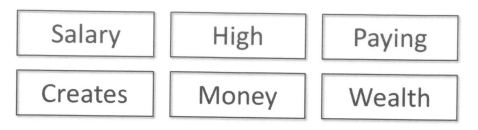

This is a classic cognitive priming task. It is a way to get participants to think about a specific topic without giving them direct instructions to that effect. So, does thinking about money change behavior? In the experiment, after unscrambling the sentences, the subject had to complete a difficult puzzle task, arranging twelve pieces into a perfect square. As the experimenter left the room, he or she said: "You can come to me if you need any help."

Who asked for help first, the money group or the neutral group? The money condition struggled with puzzle on average for five-and-a-half minutes before asking for help. The neutral condition asked for help after only about three minutes.

Being primed to think about money made participants in the money group more resistant to possible collaboration, increasingly self-reliant, and less likely to ask for help – even when they needed it. It also made them:

- Less willing to assist the experimenter in data entry
- Less willing to assist other participants who seemed confused or needed help
- Less willing to assist a stranger who spilled a box of pencils

The money group showed characteristics of business norms:

- More self-interested, resistant to collaboration, and selfish at a cost to themselves and others.
- More likely to want to spend time alone and more likely to select tasks with individual input rather than team work.

- When making decisions of where to sit, they chose seats farther away from the people they were told to collaborate with.

By contrast, research has shown that when we apply social norms in a business setting, we get greater performance and collaboration. In addition to collaboration, we also see greater loyalty to the organization. *People work harder for cause than for cash. Purpose supersedes pay.* Loyalty is created when organizations are able to connect with employees in a way that money cannot buy. Specifically, when an organization focuses on a meaningful endeavor (cause) without prioritizing immediate financial reward, loyalty to the cause and the organization is achieved.

Corporate Loyalty

If companies want to benefit from social norms, they need to cultivate a culture that appreciates social norms.

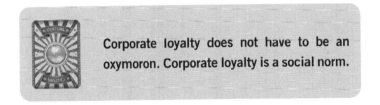

Corporate loyalty does not have to be an oxymoron. Corporate loyalty is a social norm.

Consider Google. They offer a wide variety of benefits for employees: free gourmet lunches, dry cleaning, and so on. Consider how much good will Google receives from its employees by emphasizing the social side of their relationship.

In addition, Google allows social norms to infiltrate their future business decisions. Google has a work group called Google X, run, in part, by Sergey Brin, one of Google's founders. Google X is responsible for identifying "moon shots" or high-risk, long-range projects for Google's future. These projects all must meet three criteria: (1) identify a significant problem for the world that needs solving; (2) brainstorm potential solutions; and (3) utilize breakthrough technology. As you can see, immediate profitability is not a criterion.

Those leading Google X believe that although Google X is not a philanthropic organization, it is a mistake to pick projects based on perceived profit potential. As Larry Page, co-founder of Google, says, "If a service or a product is made incrementally better, people may buy it or they may not. If you make the world a radically better place, money will find you in a fair, balanced, and elegant way."

This is why start-ups work. It's remarkable how much work a start-up company can get out of people when social norms (the excitement of building something new, together) are stronger than business norms (salaries and promotions). If you think people are only in it for the money, consider someone like Elon Musk, who made more than $100 million on the sale of PayPal. I would suggest he's not in need of more money. Yet, he has gone on to start another two companies: Tesla (electric cars) and SpaceX (private space launch vehicles). Musk draws a salary of $60,000 a year.

Another example would be Tony Hsieh, CEO of Zappos. He became wealthy through previous business endeavors, and now, as the CEO of Zappos, draws a salary of $33,000. Why such a low salary? He has stated that he doesn't want to be doing what he's doing for the money.

The last three sections have made the business case for applying social norms in a business setting. Organizations that are able to achieve this can expect better outcomes in the areas of employee performance, collaboration, and loyalty. So, how do we actually go about applying social norms in a business setting?

Implementing Social Norms in a Business Setting

Today, companies want to and need to leverage social norms. There are huge advantages to doing so with both customers and employees. Keep in mind, you can't have it both ways. You must choose which norms you will apply, and stick to those norms. Understand that there are risks and consequences of establishing social norms and then violating them.

When dealing with customers, the key to applying social norms involves establishing a genuine relationship that is mutually beneficial, rather than trying to monetize every transaction. With regard to employees, the keys to successful implementation are keeping a genuine focus on the cause of the organization and taking money off the table.

Social Norms and Customers

Businesses like to (try to) have us apply social norms in our interactions with them. They want us to think of them as family, or like we live on the same street, or they're our good friend. You can see it in many taglines, such as "Like a good neighbor, State Farm is there" or Home Depot's "You can do it, we can help."

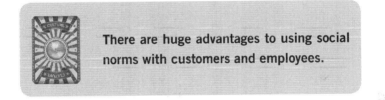

There are huge advantages to using social norms with customers and employees.

These approaches utilize a brilliant idea with potentially huge benefits. If a business and its customers are like family, the business gets several benefits, the most important of which is loyalty. Minor infractions of expectations are accommodated when social norms apply. All relationships go through their ups and downs.

Many companies have poured millions of dollars into their efforts to create social relationships with their clients. Businesses use social media in an effort to develop social norms with their customers. They clearly understand and desire the benefits that accrue to them when their customers apply social norms, but they often seem not to understand the risks and consequences of violating those social relationships.

For example, in the banking industry, what happens when a consumer bounces a check? Business norms: bank charges a fee; customer shakes it off; business is business. The fee is annoying but acceptable. Social norms: a fee rather than a waiver is like a stab in the back. It is a relationship killer. The consumer takes personal offense, leaves the bank angry, and complains endlessly to friends about how awful the bank is. Consider that years ago, if someone had a bad customer service experience, they would tell twelve people. Today, because of social media, they tell 12,000 people ... in twelve minutes.

Companies can't have it both ways. If you want a social relationship and its benefits, go for it – but remember you have to maintain it in all circumstances with human interactions. You can't treat customers as family one minute and then monetize every interaction or treat them as a number, nuisance, or competitor the next.

If you think you will have to be inflexible occasionally (for example, charging for additional time and/or services within a particular contract), don't waste your time on trying to build social norms. Have a clear value proposition (e.g., *quid pro quo*) that specifies what you give and what you expect in return. Not setting up social norms and expectations is a good way to ensure you don't violate them. It's just business, nothing more.

With customers, the critical components of applying social norms are establishing a genuine relationship that is mutually beneficial to both the organization and the customer, as well as not needing to monetize every transaction. We see similar themes in the application of social norms with employees, two key components being focusing on the cause of the organization and taking money off the table.

Social Norms and Employees

Historically, the negotiated contract between employee and employer was that the employee would work 9-5 in exchange for a paycheck. This was a clear business exchange that worked adequately for both sides. However, in today's market, employees are looking for more than a paycheck.

> Social norms define a critical part of the culture we cultivate. They are the soil in which we plant the seeds of our organizational culture.

As demonstrated in the first chapter, organizations have a tendency to overemphasize personality traits and individual skills when hiring, promoting, and training employees. We also learned that culture has an enormous influence on biology, psychology, and ultimately, performance. The key to establishing a culture that drives performance with employees is to apply social norms.

I'm not suggesting that organizations should ignore individual employee characteristics and skills. But, even if you happen to find someone with what you consider ideal skills and characteristics, why will they want to work for you? What will get them to stay? Salary? If so, why wouldn't they just leave when they are offered a higher salary somewhere else? In truth, if money is the draw, they may go to work for you but will soon leave you for an organization that pays more.

> Money is the most expensive way to motivate people, and it does so only in the short term. Social norms are not only cheaper, but they last longer and are more effective.

This concept, that you can create a culture based on social norms when you take money off the table, comes straight from Maslow's Hierarchy of Needs and is illustrated clearly in low-wage jobs. When a person is struggling to make ends meet, when they have difficulty paying for housing and/or food, they will always jump to the next higher-paying job. But when we pay people a living wage that is fair and competitive, one where employees don't have to struggle for basic needs, then we can offer them meaning, purpose, and cause. Then, they will stay because of the culture of social norms.

Today, creativity is more important than it was during the Industrial Revolution. The line separating work and home has been blurred. People running the workplace want us to think about work on the drive home and in the shower. The laptop and smartphone bridge the gap between work and home. Companies are going from hourly to monthly pay.

In a blended work environment, social norms provide an advantage. If you want employees to think like entrepreneurial owners, then apply social norms. Social norms are what make employees more passionate, hard-working, flexible, and concerned. Social norms are the way to make employees loyal and motivated.

Consider, for example, open source software. Linux is an operating system that allows you to post a problem and see how fast others react to your request for assistance. You could pay for this type of technical support, but it would cost you a major body part.

People in social norm communities are happy to offer their time and expertise to society at large, as they get the same social benefits we all get from helping a friend paint their house.

Even in cultures where social norms are applied, high performers are still recognized and rewarded, just as they are in cultures with business norms. The difference lies in the types of rewards that are applied in a culture with social norms. Specifically, in order to remain within social norms, rewards are not monetized.

Social Norms and Rewards

Too often, companies look to offer financial rewards to their employees for a job well done. What are often overlooked are the influential rewards available through social norms. Once money is taken off the table, these often serve as much more powerful motivators of behavior than monetary rewards, and they are infrequently used. Four of the most powerful social norm rewards include:

Praise: acknowledgment of a job well done
Gratitude: genuine expression of thankfulness
Recognition: acknowledgment of outstanding performance
Reputation: spreading the word about outstanding performance

When a company moves to create a culture using social norms, they must understand there is a tacit long-term commitment. If an employee promises to work harder to achieve an important and difficult deadline – even canceling family obligations to do so   the employee must get something in return. If an employee is asked to travel at a moment's notice to attend a meeting, the employee must get something in return – and it doesn't have to be a bonus check!

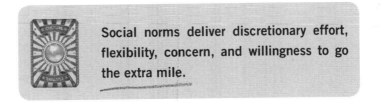

Social norms deliver discretionary effort, flexibility, concern, and willingness to go the extra mile.

The employee should receive something like support when s/he or a family member is sick, kudos for their sacrifice, a sense of improved reputation, or a chance to hold onto his or her job when the market threatens to take the job away.

In social exchanges, if something goes wrong, people believe that the other party's intention is noble and that he or she will be there for them, to protect and help them. You won't find that in any employment contract, but there is a general sense of obligation, that we are all in this together, and we will provide help and support in times of need.

As important and effective as intangible rewards can be towards driving performance in a culture that uses social norms, there are tangible, non-monetized rewards that can also be used.

Gifts can work as a strong incentive, particularly if they are personalized, because they remain part of a social norm. But, if you mention how much the gift costs, you introduce it as a business norm. People will work harder for a reasonable wage and for free. Offer just a small payment, and they will walk away. Gifts keep us in the realm of social norms.

In order to get people to focus on the cause of the organization, we must pay people fairly, competitively, and at a level that will allow them to live a comfortable lifestyle. People work harder for cause than for cash, when you take the issue of money off the table. Discretionary effort and increased performance come from cause more than cash.

In a study conducted by Dan Ariely and his colleagues, referenced earlier in this chapter, we saw that subjects performed much better on a simple task when social norms were invoked (doing the task as a favor for the experimenter) versus when business norms were invoked (various payment schemes for performance). In a subsequent experiment,[3] Stephan Kossmeier, Dan Ariely, and Anat Bracha repeated the same experiment (moving circles inside squares), only this time looking at gifts as the reward. The rewards were:

Group 1:   Godiva chocolates that cost five dollars (price mentioned)
Group 2:   Snickers bars that cost fifty cents (price mentioned)
Group 3:   Godiva chocolates (no mention of price)
Group 4:   Snickers bars (no mention of price)

What were the results?

Group 1:   moved 117 circles
Group 2:   moved 116 circles

Group 3: moved 163 circles

Group 4: moved 165 circles

These results demonstrate that, just as with the previous experiment, social norms are more powerful motivators than business norms. This time, groups three and four performed basically equally. Both were given chocolate as gifts, with no mention of the cost. If you mention the market price, you get business norm behavior. If you do not, you get social norm behavior. For business norms to emerge and prevail, all that is necessary is the mention of money, even when no actual money changes hands.

Think about how people respond to a thoughtful gift with a value of $1000, versus simply handing over $1000 in cash. Most employees might say they prefer the cash, but the gift is what they will remember – especially if it is meaningful or thoughtful. The gift, in addition to its monetary value, provides a boost in the social relationship between employer and employee and provides long-term benefits to everyone.

Several years ago, I was consulting for a company that sold financial products. The salespeople were all individual performers who worked primarily with a small salary and a large commission based on sales over the course of the year. My consulting contract began six months after a new CEO had been brought in by the board. The CEO realized that for many of his salespeople, once they met their personal financial needs, often in the late second or early third quarter, they appeared less driven (fewer calls, fewer trips to see clients, fewer sales closed in the second half of the year).

The CEO thought this was odd because in his experience, most salespeople he had known were motivated by more money and more commission. So, in order to try to incentivize higher performance towards the end of the year, in September of that year, the CEO informed his sales force that there would be a "Top Sales" award announced at the annual holiday party. Sales increased a modest 5% towards the end of the year. At the annual holiday party, with much fanfare, the CEO announced the Top Sales Person award went to John, along with a bonus of $50,000. Applause and congratulations followed, and by all appearances it had gone well.

But it had not.

John was a successful salesperson who, like most of his colleagues, was hitting his personal financial goals between the second and third quarter of every year. Unlike most of his colleagues, however, he was an introvert. This means that when his name was announced and he was called up to receive the award, he was mortified. He was displeased with the process (being singled out and called up in public), and while grateful for the bonus, it was not particularly motivating to him, as he had already met his financial goals for the year.

Towards the end of the following year, sales were up modestly again (5%), and John once again was in a position to win the "Top Sales" award, based on his sales numbers. The CEO remembered clearly what had happened the year before when he presented John with the award at the annual holiday party, and he did not want to repeat the same mistake. In subsequent conversations, we discussed the fact that John was an introvert and very much a family man. He didn't want or need the extra attention, and the additional bonus, while appreciated, had not been a particular motivator for any of the salespeople, as evidenced by the modest increase of 5%.

Using knowledge of the power of gifts, we took a different path than the one taken the preceding year. For that year's award, we contacted John's wife, Christina, letting her know that John had won the "Top Sales" award again this year, but this year we wanted to do something very special for him. We asked her to keep it a secret. She agreed. We then asked her to provide us with a variety of pictures of John, herself, and their two children. Those pictures were then taken to a local, well-known artist who created a family portrait from the pictures provided. The cost of the painting (which was not shared with anyone) was $10,000.

On the day of the holiday party, at the end of the day, John was called into the CEO's office on his way out. The CEO came out from behind the desk, shook his hand and let him know he was again the winner of the "Top Sales" award. John winced a bit thinking that he was going to be identified again in a very public forum that evening, but the CEO simply expressed his gratitude and pointed to the corner of his office where, wrapped in paper, was the painting. As John opened the painting and realized it was a portrait of his family, his eyes welled up with tears, and he turned to the CEO and actually hugged him! He expressed his gratitude profusely.

At the holiday dinner that night, the CEO did announce the "Top Sales" award had gone to John (but did not require him to come to the podium) and mentioned that the award came with a family portrait painted by the well-known local artist. John was brimming with pride, as was his family. He was showing others pictures of the portrait that he had taken with his phone.

The next year, in the third and fourth quarter, sales jumped 20% over previous years. The painting, which had cost the company one-fifth of the cash bonus, had quadrupled the sales performance. Why? There was a recognition by the sales team that this CEO was invested in providing rewards that reflected deep personal significance and meaning to top performers, in the form of something they were unlikely to purchase for themselves.

A gift is a gesture; no one will work for gifts rather than salary. However, when we pay our employees fairly, competitively and at a level that allows them to live a particular lifestyle, we get extraordinary effort and performance. Taking money off the table allows employees to focus on social norms.

Cultivating a culture that is focused on social norms clearly requires significant effort but carries with it significant advantages, such as employee performance, collaboration, and loyalty. Although these are benefits we all seek, it is important to understand that, like a garden, a culture of social norms requires maintenance and vigilance to ensure that weeds – in the form of business norms or other detrimental behavioral norms – are not allowed to sneak back in and take root. If business norms are introduced into a culture that is focused on social norms, the benefits of social norms are quickly lost and are extremely difficult to reestablish.

Business Norms vs. Social Norms: A Cautionary Tale

When business norms collide with social norms, social norms tend to lose. Social relationships are not easy to reestablish. Once lost, it takes a great deal of time, patience, and investment for social norms to return.

In a naturalistic experiment done in Israel, Uri Gneezy of the Israel Institue of Technology and Aldo Rustichini of the Center for Economic Research, were able to look at the long-term effects of switching from social norms to business norms.[4]

These researchers worked with a day care center in Israel that was trying to get parents to pick up their children in a timely manner. The day care center was trying to determine whether imposing a fine on parents who were late to pick up their children would be a useful deterrent and/or if it would change the parents' behavior.

Before any fine was imposed, teachers and parents were involved in a strong social contract with social norms around caring for the children and the importance of being there to pick up their children on time. If parents were late, as they were occasionally, they felt guilty (an emotion which is probably a very good influencer of behavior in many countries). It was the guilt that compelled them to make greater efforts to be on time in the future.

In an effort to try to reduce parent tardiness further, the day care center decided to impose a fine for those parents who picked up their children after the designated time. Once the fine was imposed, the day care effectively replaced the social norms with business norms. Did the parents' behavior change? Yes, it absolutely did. Since parents were now paying for being late, they could decide on their own to be late or not. The frequency of late pick-ups by parents actually *increased*.

Because this behavior was not in the direction that the day care center had wanted or anticipated, they decided to remove the fine. This is where it gets interesting. The day care center removed the fine in an effort to return to social norms, allowing the parents' guilt to influence their behavior. Did the parents go back to applying social norms? No.

When the fine was imposed, the problem behavior increased because parents felt they were "buying" the extra time (business norm). Once the effort was made to return to social norms, the frequency of late pick-ups did not return to previous levels. Late pick-ups remained high.

Once social norms, which are much more powerful motivators than business norms, are replaced by business norms, it is very hard to reestablish social norms. Once the relationship of a social norm is displaced by a business norm, it is difficult to recapture.

Business Norms, Social Norms, and Motivation

Businesses can always raise people's salaries to try to make them more willing to give up more of their time, but how much will that cost? Alternatively, businesses can increase the focus on social norms. If businesses can make people feel that they are doing a job with meaning, a real mission, a purpose, or a cause (worth much more than base pay), then they are applying social norms. Let employees know that they are doing a job that has a real impact on the world. We must honor employees, not only for a job well done, but also for their contributions to the organization and to society. This takes an inspirational, cause-driven culture.

If companies start thinking in terms of social norms, they will learn that these norms build loyalty and make people want to extend themselves in ways that businesses need today (discretionary effort, flexibility, concern, ownership mentality, willingness to go the extra mile). If you and your business want to get this kind of productivity and effort from your employees, consider asking the following questions:

1. Does your business focus on business norms or social norms?
2. Do your employees think in terms of dollar signs rather than the social value you provide as a business?

3. Does your organization receive the loyalty, commitment, and creativity it needs?

So What?

Will people put their lives on the line for business norms or social norms? Do fire fighters run into a burning building or protect structures from wild fires because they will get some bonus pay? Did the teachers in Moore, Oklahoma, in the summer of 2013, who threw themselves over their students when a tornado struck, do so because it was in their contract or because they thought they would earn an additional bonus?

Firefighting and teaching, as well as the military, law enforcement, and many other service-oriented professions, are examples of professions that focus on social norms to achieve peak performance. None of the people in these jobs are willing to put their lives at risk simply for their (often painfully low) salaries.

Their behavior is explained by social norms: they have pride in their profession, a sense of honor, a sense of duty, and a connection to others. This is the type of dedication all organizations are looking to create among their employees. Social norms deliver discretionary effort, flexibility, concern, and a willingness to go the extra mile.

Despite the tendency in many organizations to use money as the go-to strategy for solving performance issues, money remains the most expensive and often least effective way to motivate people. Social norms are not only cheaper, but they last longer and are more effective. This means that if organizations want to maximize employee performance, they must move to create a culture of social norms by focusing on intangibles (praise, gratitude, recognition, and reputation) and tangibles in the form of highly valued and personalized (yet non-monetized) rewards.

Taking Action

If I were coming to your place of work for the very first time, and I called to tell you that I'm totally lost, the first question you would ask me would be, "Where are you?"

To find out where you need to go, you need to start by identifying where you are. Consider:

1. Do you currently have a culture of primarily business norms or primarily social norms in your organization? How can you tell?
2. What is the primary motivator for you personally? Money or cause?
3. What are you currently trying to do in order to motivate your employees?
4. What can you do in the next 30 days to begin to establish stronger social norms in your organization?

CHAPTER 3

CORPORATE MODELS

"Always place principles before profits, not profits
before principles, in all engagements."

– Constance Chuks Friday,
Author

What You Need To Know:

1. The business models of the Industrial Revolution no longer work in our post-industrial information age and knowledge economy.

2. A successful future business model will move beyond mechanical models and build a culture that will consider and embrace multiple constituencies.

3. The words of senior leaders are hollow and meaningless if they themselves are unwilling to live by the standards of the culture they espouse.

4. Members of an organization will take their lead, or cues about what actions to take behaviorally, from the organization's culture before considering "policy" or "stated" behavioral guidelines.

5. A company must focus on its stakeholders, not just its shareholders. Building a culture that considers and embraces stakeholders also yields greater profit.

6. The Happiness Paradox: people don't strive to do things to achieve happiness; happiness results from doing things.

7. The Profit Paradox: in business, long-term profits are best achieved by *not* making profit the primary goal of your business.

8. Great causes lead to great profit. Profit is a result of efficient performance. When the cause comes first, profit follows.

9. Social capitalism will reward those companies that build cultures that connect with society as a whole, understanding that profits will follow.

10. Companies that focus on culture create value for all their stakeholders and offer exceptional stock market returns in both the near and long term, in addition to building long-term loyalty from employees, customers, vendors, and investors.

11. The consumer-driven, zero-sum game, materialistic society is shifting to a society focused on experiencing connections between beings. This connection comes from the organizational culture that focuses on how each company interacts with its stakeholders, not just stockholders.

There are many business models that lead to profit. Some go back as far as the Industrial Revolution; some more modern models were created for a post-industrial, knowledge-based economy. This chapter will discuss some of these different models and focus on, in particular, the differences between two well-known companies, Enron and Zappos, and how within each company culture drives (and drove) behavior.

 The business models of the Industrial Revolution no longer work in our post-industrial information age and knowledge economy.

Social proof argues that members of an organization will determine what actions to take behaviorally, from the organization's culture, before considering "policy" or "stated" behavioral guidelines. There is a great deal of research, including much of this book, that supports the assertion that culture drives behavior. This chapter shows that, for the most successful companies, culture and people come before profit. Profit-driven companies are actually less profitable than culture-driven companies. Culture trumps everything.

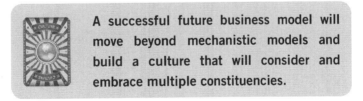 A successful future business model will move beyond mechanistic models and build a culture that will consider and embrace multiple constituencies.

Enron Beginning

In 1932, a natural gas company was formed in Omaha, Nebraska. It was called the Northern Natural Gas Company. After 47 years of successful operation, it was reorganized. In 1979, it became the main subsidiary of a holding company, InterNorth, which was a diversified energy and energy-related products company.

InterNorth was a major player in natural gas production, transmission, and marketing, as well as for natural gas liquids. It was also an innovator in the plastics industry, owned the company Peak Antifreeze, and developed EVAL resins for food packaging.

When a company such as Northern Natural Gas Company has a 47-year history of success, it is safe to argue it has a well-established culture. When companies reorganize or are bought and sold, those companies, and the people who inhabit them, go through a shift in culture.

In 1985, when InterNorth bought the smaller and less diversified Houston Natural Gas Company, the new company was initially named HNG/InterNorth Inc., even though InterNorth was the nominal parent. It built a large and lavish headquarters complex with pink marble in Omaha (known locally as the Pink Palace). As often happens, six months after the HNG/InterNorth merger, the original CEO, Samuel Segnar, stepped down to allow the next CEO to ascend. His name, which would later become (in)famous, was Kenneth Lay. The company would soon become known as Enron.

At its peak, 1996-2001, Enron was an energy, commodities, and services company employing nearly 22,000 people. Based in Houston, Texas, Enron was one of the largest energy companies in the world. It had been named "America's Most Innovative Company" for six consecutive years by *Fortune* magazine. The company was regarded as a competitive, talent-focused culture where "stars" were lavishly rewarded and were then permitted to have the autonomy to launch new projects.

In hindsight, the first sign of trouble was the creation of a 64-page book called The Enron Ethics Manual. This was a clear indication that someone was concerned about the motivations underlying decision making within the organization. This concern ultimately proved well-founded.

The Ethics Manual

By any measure, The Enron Code of Ethics manual was a colossal effort that went well beyond other corporate ethics guidelines that are typically framed and hung on any business' wall. This 64-page manual not only outlined the company's mission and core values, but also the various ethical policies that all employees were expected to follow.

Consider that while a variety of companies draft mission statements, vision statements, and core values manuals and handbooks, for most they seem to serve as guidelines to acceptable and unacceptable behaviors in the organization. Most of these statements are created in similar ways, with senior leadership attending an off-site meeting or series of meetings where various drafts of the guidelines are defined and wordsmithed until the final guidelines are created.

These guidelines and statements are later used for the purpose of organizational or institutional training in the hope that the words and the spirit of the statements will be extended to the behavior of the employees.

For Enron, a core component of the ethic manual was the articulation of Enron's four core values.

Enron listed its core values as follows:

1. *Communication*: We have an obligation to communicate.
2. *Respect*: We treat others as we would like to be treated.
3. *Integrity*: We work with customers and prospects openly, honestly, and sincerely.
4. *Excellence*: We are satisfied with nothing less than the very best in everything we do.

Although these sound very nice and read well as part of their 64-page ethics manual, the behavioral and cultural reality at Enron was very different.

Social Proof at Enron: Actions Speak Louder than Words

For all the talk and documentation of ethics, the reality on the ground was vastly different. This became painfully evident as the organization began to unravel, and more and more information about the internal operations of the organization became public.

 The words of senior leaders are hollow and meaningless if they themselves are unwilling to live by the standards of the culture they espouse.

Kenneth Lay began to set the culture through social proof soon after he became CEO. For starters, he relocated the company's headquarters to Houston after promising to keep it in Omaha. He also began to change the business and its practices. Almost immediately after the relocation to Houston, Enron began selling major assets such as its chemicals division, Northern PetroChemicals; accepted silent partners in Enron CoGeneration, Northern Border Pipeline and Transwestern Pipeline; and became a less diversified company. Early financial analysts said Enron was accumulating great debt and the sale of major operations would not solve the problem.

The CEO that succeeded Kenneth Lay, Jeffrey Skilling, having taken inspiration from a book called *The Selfish Gene*, established a grading system for all employees. Rather than train or coach those that had performance challenges, he summarily fired those he believed had failed to help the company meet its performance targets, which were directly tied to his own compensation.

This culture of greed was furthered during the tenure of one of Enron's Chief Financial Officers, Andrew Fastow, who was also on the company's Board of Directors. In his efforts to continue to grow revenue on Enron's balance sheet, Fastow established Special Partnership Entities, where he could separate and uniquely bundle different assets and liabilities. This allowed him to hide liabilities, show greater assets, and continue to secure loans from financial institutions. The Board of Enron, fully aware of Fastow's involvement in these partnerships, and also aware that these actions were a violation of its code of ethics (Communication, Respect, Integrity), voted to suspend the application of the code of ethics to Fastow.

These actions of senior leaders clearly shaped the culture at Enron. This becomes clear when one reads reports from energy traders for Enron who were bragging to each other about the various tactics they were using during the California blackouts. They would routinely decrease supply and increase demand for energy in order to increase the price of energy. This created widespread rolling blackouts and brownouts throughout California that were more than just a minor inconvenience. The blackouts and brownouts caused distress for large institutions, such as hospitals and child care centers, as well as the elderly. Internally at Enron, there was awareness about these behaviors, but no one spoke out against them.

> **Members of an organization will take their lead, or cues about what actions to take behaviorally, from the organization's culture before considering "policy" or "stated" behavioral guidelines.**

The actions of the leadership at Enron demonstrated greed and selfishness, and its employees followed suit. Although respect and integrity were part of Enron's core values, the leadership's behaviors – or social proof – did not support or demonstrate those values. The words of senior leaders are hollow and meaningless if they themselves are unwilling to live by the standards of culture they espouse. The behaviors of a leadership team best demonstrate and establish cultural behavioral norms, regardless of policies, vision, and mission statements. This is social proof in action.

Not all companies function the Enron way, but those that do typically will meet the same end. Fortunately, there are other business models that demonstrate greater long-term success and profit through social proof. Zappos serves as a strong contrast to Enron and demonstrates how social proof can foster positive behaviors, rather than negative ones.

Zappos Beginning

Zappos was founded as an online shoe retailer by Nick Swinmurn in 1999. His inspiration came when he could not find a pair of brown Airwalks at his local mall. Later that year, Swinmurn approached two venture capitalists, Tony Hsieh and Alfred Lin, proposing that they help him sell shoes online. Hsieh was initially skeptical of the idea, until Swinmurn showed Hsieh that at the time the footwear industry in the US was a $40 billion market and 5% of that was already being sold by mail order catalogs.

Through their investment firm, Venture Frogs, Hsieh and Lin invested $2 million. The company was officially launched in June 1999 under the original domain name ShoeSite.com. A few months after the initial launch, the company's name and website were changed from ShoeSite to Zappos (a variation of "zapatos," the Spanish word for "shoes"). They already had larger plans for selling products beyond footwear. After minimal gross sales in 1999, Zappos brought in $1.6 million in revenue in 2000. In 2009, Amazon acquired Zappos in a stock deal worth $1.2 billion.

Since its inception, Zappos has continuously expanded its product offerings and now also sells clothing, accessories, and even various overstocked merchandise through its subsidiary companies. In comparison to Enron, Zappos is a small company. It employs just over 2,000 people at its headquarters in Las Vegas, Nevada, and in its warehouse in Kentucky. But size is only the beginning of the difference. More importantly, Zappos differs greatly in business philosophy and culture.

The company emphasizes the importance of its culture and its values, focusing on the happiness of both its employees and its customers. When a company puts emphasis on employee engagement and customer satisfaction, profit invariably follows.

Zappos' Core Values

Interestingly, in contrast to Enron's 64-page ethics manual, Zappos did not make any effort to codify its culture or core values for the first six years after its inception. Tony Hsieh, Zappos' CEO, believed strongly that writing out core values was too corporate and ineffective.

He was quite familiar with the offsite retreat homework assignment used by most corporations, drafted by leadership with no input from employees, and did not want to draft a document that failed to reflect the true culture of his employees. Instead, he focused first on creating a compelling company culture, with a commitment to exceptional customer experiences.

In 2010, Hsieh reinforced this culture by putting together a book of essays about company culture comprised entirely of employee contributions. Zappos then developed training programs designed to reinforce this internal framework.

It was actually Zappos employees that persuaded Hsieh that they needed a statement of values to represent the Zappos culture. Rather than gathering his senior executives at an off-site to prepare a statement of values, Hsieh returned to the strategy that worked so well in creating the Zappos culture book. He emailed everyone in the company, asking for their input on what they believed were the core values of Zappos. In other words, Hsieh's approach was a bottom-up approach rather than Enron's top-down approach. This served to codify Zappos' culture based on behaviors employees already saw, exhibited, and considered important (social proof). The Zappos culture continues to serve as an inspiration for others to follow.

Like a gardener lovingly tending to his plants, Hsieh then pruned and watered certain ideas, combining similar values and expanding on others. Finally, they settled on ten core values:

1. Deliver WOW through Service.
2. Embrace and Drive Change.
3. Create Fun and a Little Weirdness.
4. Be Adventurous, Creative, and Open-Minded.
5. Pursue Growth and Learning.
6. Build Open and Honest Relationships with Communication.
7. Build a Positive Team and Family Spirit.
8. Do More with Less.
9. Be Passionate and Determined.
10. Be Humble.

These core values remain unchanged today. Once identified, Hsieh knew he had to ensure they were well-rooted in the organization. To do so, the Human Resources department created specific interview questions to ensure that, through the application of behavioral interviewing (a thorough examination on candidates' beliefs and experiences with each of these core values), the best candidates would be selected.

The successful candidate who was hired read and signed a statement of acknowledgement, indicating their understanding and acceptance of the company's core values. Zappos goes as far as offering to pay employees to quit, in the first 30 days, if they do not fit into its culture, believing it is more economical to pay someone who doesn't fit to leave, than it is to pay someone on an ongoing basis who will not perform, fit or adapt into the existing culture.

Keep in mind, one principle distinction between Enron and Zappos is that Zappos leadership did not lead with a statement of core values. Instead, Hsieh created and reinforced specific behaviors that formed part of a culture that demonstrated specific values and desired behavioral norms. Employees later identified those values based on their experience in the Zappos culture.

Social Proof at Zappos: Actions Still Speak Louder than Words

The way that Zappos' leadership went about creating its culture not only created a list of values that employees already believed in, but also leveraged the power of social proof to ensure that employees identified and acted on what they believe.

One of the greatest challenges of Zappos' beliefs and culture came when 6pm.com, a bargain shoes, clothing, accessories, and electronics website that Zappos had purchased in 2007, accidentally priced all their merchandise at $49.95, including items like GPS navigators and other electronics worth much more.

It took Zappos employees more than six hours to find and correct the error. After the error was found and corrected, Zappos' Director of Brand Marketing and Business Development made an announcement on the company's blog: Zappos would honor every transaction. This decision would cost Zappos over $1.6 million, but it would also serve as another example of how Zappos sought to stay true to its culture and core values and "Deliver WOW through Service."

The Happiness Paradox

For most CEOs, there is a desire or inclination to run directly towards this future model of cultural and financial success. As we all remember from high school geometry, the shortest distance between two points is a straight line.

However, there is a paradox inherent in the model. This paradox stems from the fact that profit comes from not directly pursuing it. Instead, profit results as a consequence of doing those things that allow profit to naturally result.

This is much like the research in the field of happiness where it has been demonstrated that happiness cannot be pursued directly as a goal in and of itself. Instead, happiness results as a consequence of doing those things that allow happiness to naturally result.

With his article published in 1998, Martin Seligman, a psychologist at the University of Pennsylvania, began a new field of psychological research referred to as "positive psychology."[1] After many years of studying clinical depression, its dysfunction, and its treatment, Seligman began to look at positive psychology as the study of positive emotions such as happiness and the behaviors that lead to happiness and a more fulfilling life.

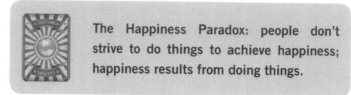

The Happiness Paradox: people don't strive to do things to achieve happiness; happiness results from doing things.

Seligman and positive psychology research have given us the following correlational findings. Humans seem happiest when they experience:

- *Pleasure* (tasty food, warm baths, etc.)
- *Engagement* (the absorption of an enjoyable, yet challenging, activity; often referred to as "the flow experience")
- *Relationships* (social ties are one of the most reliable indicators of happiness)
- *Meaning* (a perceived quest or belonging to something bigger)
- *Accomplishments* (having realized tangible goals)

PERMA is the widely used acronym to describe the five factors that are associated with happiness – but, like profit, happiness also has a paradox.

Interestingly, those people who spend their life trying to achieve the PERMA concepts for self-interest are often perceived as being self-involved and narcissistic. More importantly, these people often find that, throughout their lives, happiness eludes them, almost as if mocking them. As they reach the end of their lives, they are often depressed and alone, regardless of their wealth or socioeconomic status.

As we are told by positive psychology, happiness is the result of experiencing pleasure from the things around us without making them our primary focus. Feeling engagement as experienced by flow of a challenging activity; building significant relationships with those around us; experiencing meaning through belonging to things larger than ourselves; and realizing accomplishments through the experience of setting and achieving goals. People don't strive to do these things to achieve happiness; happiness results from doing these things. This is the happiness paradox.

The Profit Paradox

In business, profits display a similar paradox. Long-term profits are best achieved not by making them the primary goal of your business. Long-term profits are a result of having a business cause, producing a great product, having engaged employees and committed and loyal customers, developing collaborative relationships with supply partners, and demonstrating concern for the community and the environment. These are the complex constituencies social capitalism requires businesses to consider in order to create profit. This is the profit paradox. The profit paradox is that, like happiness, profits are best achieved by not making them your primary goal, but by focusing on the behaviors that lead to profit.

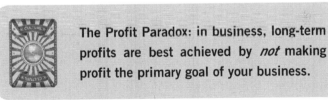

The Profit Paradox: in business, long-term profits are best achieved by *not* making profit the primary goal of your business.

This also defines the shift that must occur from industrial models of business to social capitalism business models. The industrial model of profit – where the production factors (capital, labor, land) combine in the right blend and lead to profit – no longer works. In the social capitalism business model, leadership and management work collaboratively to create a self-adaptive, self-sustaining culture that takes into account all of the business' interdependent constituencies.

Businesses with cultures that are able to evolve in a self-adaptive way become self-sustaining through naturalistic rewards coming from all constituencies (owners, investors, leaders, managers, employees, customers, suppliers, community, etc.) and become the most successful as measured by long-term profit.

The most common counterargument to the paragraph above is that there are thousands of businesses whose only concern is classical capitalism. These businesses focus on applying industrial mechanistic business models to maximize profit for owners and investors without taking into account culture or the interdependencies of the modern era.

These models reflect traditional views of organizations and societies that were developed more than 200 years ago. At that time, organizations and society were very different.

Economic Models

Early economic models did not consider culture as a significant economic or organizational factor. In 1776, Adam Smith wrote *The Wealth of Nations*,[2] which uses mechanical metaphors to explain how companies and the economy operate. Smith famously discussed the economic trinity of labor, land, and capital as what he called "factors of production." This model states that business operates like a machine. It is the responsibility of ownership to provide adequate capital, labor, and land at the beginning of this mechanistic process. The machine of business takes these "factors of production," and, at the end of the process, produces profit. In this model, the purpose of business is to convert factors of production (labor, land, and capital) into profit for the benefit of owners and investors.

These mechanical metaphors are outdated because they are less profitable than other, more modern and holistic approaches; they feed and inform the negative perceptions of business; and they also fail to take into account that our society is well into a post-industrial, knowledge economy. Today, business constituencies extend far beyond simply business owners and investors.

Industrial-age models fail in today's world because they fail to appreciate the interdependencies of diverse consumers and their evolving concerns and interests. Today, consumers care about a company's cause or purpose; where products come from, how they were made, if any person or animal was harmed in the manufacturing process; and what the company is doing to support, help, or improve the environment, just to name a few concerns that mechanical models do not consider.

The successful future business will move beyond mechanical models and build a culture that will consider and embrace cause as well as these multiple constituencies. This is the reality in which corporations and society live today. This is also the basis of "social capitalism," a rising new economic model. Social capitalism describes companies that strive, through communication and action, to endear themselves to all of their primary stakeholders (customers, employees, partners, communities, and shareholders). These companies understand that when culture, cause, and social capitalism come first, profit follows. These companies align the interests of all the stakeholders so that no one group gains at the expense of another; one does not "take advantage" of another.

The good news is that building a culture that considers and embraces cause and an organization's complex constituencies yields greater profit. Cause is the fundamental driver of social capitalism; profit is its indirect result.

Cause Drives Greater Profit

In March of 1999, Elon Musk started X.com, an online financial services and e-mail payment company, because of his belief in emerging online person-to-person transfer or "P2P" technology. One year later, X.com acquired Confinity, which operated an auction payment system similar in size to X.com. It was called PayPal. The combined company at first adopted X.com as the corporate name, but in February of 2001, X.com changed its legal name to PayPal Inc.

Because of his belief in P2P, Musk was instrumental in PayPal's new focus on a global payment system and departure from the core financial offerings of X.com. PayPal's early growth was due in large part to a successful viral growth campaign created by Musk. In October of 2002, PayPal Inc. was acquired by eBay for $1.5 billion in stock. Before its sale, Musk was the company's largest shareholder, owning 11.7% of PayPal's shares, meaning in the transaction he made approximately $175 million.

But it was not the money that drove Musk; it was his belief in changing the world. If Musk was motivated by money, he might have sat back and relaxed after a $175 million payday (as many of us might be tempted to do). He did not.

Cause Drives SpaceX

In June of 2002, Musk founded a third company – Space Exploration Technologies – better known as SpaceX. SpaceX develops and manufactures space launch vehicles with a focus on advancing the state of rocket technology. The company's first two launch vehicles are the Falcon 1 and Falcon 9 rockets, and its first spacecraft is called Dragon.

SpaceX was awarded a $1.6 billion NASA contract on December 23, 2008, for twelve flights of their Falcon 9 rocket and Dragon spacecraft to the International Space Station, replacing the Space Shuttle after it was retired in 2011. This contract, which has a minimum value of $1.6 billion and a maximum value of $3.1 billion, has become a cornerstone of the Space Station's continued access to cargo delivery and return.

After making $175 million on the sale of PayPal, why start SpaceX? Musk believes space exploration is an important step in expanding and preserving human life. Musk has said that multi-planetary life may serve as a hedge against threats to the survival of the human species. Musk has also said, "An asteroid or a super volcano could destroy us, and we face risks the dinosaurs never saw: an engineered virus, inadvertent creation of a micro black hole, catastrophic global warming or some as-yet-unknown technology could spell the end of us. Humankind evolved over millions of years, but in the last sixty years atomic weaponry created the potential to extinguish ourselves. Sooner or later, we must expand life beyond this green and blue ball—or go extinct."

In the coming years, Musk will focus on delivering astronauts to the International Space Station, but has stated his personal goal of eventually enabling human exploration and settlement of Mars. In a 2011 interview, he said he hopes to send humans to Mars' surface within 10–20 years.

Because Musk is driven by causes beyond money, he also was a part of starting both Tesla Motors, an electric car company, and SolarCity, the largest provider of photovoltaic systems in the United States. Musk's underlying motivation for funding both SolarCity and Tesla is to help combat global climate change. In 2012, Musk announced that SolarCity and Tesla Motors are collaborating to use electric vehicle batteries to modulate the flow of electricity to and from the power grid. In 2014, Musk "released" all the patents previously held by Tesla Motors. In essence, Musk is sharing Tesla Motors' advanced battery technology with the world in an effort to combat climate change by reducing the use of fossil fuels worldwide.

> Great causes lead to great profit. Profit is a result of efficient performance. When the cause comes first, profit follows.

Musk has built his companies with a strong cause. Even through the Great Recession, his companies continued to grow and prosper. It is because of culture and cause that he has been successful. It is because of culture and cause that his companies will continue to be successful.

Musk and his companies are just one example of how cause is an important component of social capitalism. However, his companies are not the only examples. The next section will compare the financial performance of a variety of social capitalism companies to the financial performance of classic capitalism companies. The results suggest that there is a major transformation of business models on the horizon.

Profit Comparison: Classic Capitalism vs. Social Capitalism

As a result of their groundbreaking research, Rajendra Sisodia, David Wolfe, and Jagdish Sheth published *Firms of Endearment: How World-Class Companies Profit from Passion and Purpose.*[3] The authors argue that we are entering the "Age of Transcendence" because of our aging Baby Boomers searching for meaning and belonging to things larger than themselves: a cause rather than just more material possessions. They describe a social transformation within capitalism that begins with culture and impacts people of every generation.

 Social capitalism will reward those companies that build cultures that connect with society as a whole, understanding that profits will follow.

The executives that run these companies see their role as not only running a company but also being a powerful catalyst for associating a human side to capitalism. They create cultures that people are proud to do business with, proud to partner with, proud to work for, and proud to invest in. They see themselves as stewards of the organization, where profits are invested (in employees, customers, and systems) for additional growth and purpose, in contrast to owners and/or investors who too often view employees as an expense line item in a budget.

In addition to creating cultures where all stakeholders are important, leaders of companies that operate through social capitalism define a cause for their organizations. Great causes lead to great profit (as long as the work is done effectively and efficiently, and driven with stakeholders in mind). Profit is a result of efficient performance. When the cause comes first, profit follows.

In most cases, businesses come from an idea that feeds or informs its purpose or cause. Before a single dime is ever invested, the business purpose or cause is defined by an entrepreneur's desire to change the world or change human experience in the world in some way. This is the fundamental purpose or cause for any business. It is this cause that too often gets lost in the pursuit of profit (social norms being pushed out by business norms). I am not suggesting that a company can forego or ignore profitability. Profit to a business is like breathing to a human. It is necessary for life, but it in no way defines a meaningful life.

I am stating that greater profit is a result of a focus on social capitalism. This is made most clear when looking directly at companies that focus on social capitalism.

Social Capitalism Will Win the Future

Social capitalism is demonstrated by companies that align the interests of all of their complex constituencies so that no single group takes advantage of or gains at the expense of another. They strive through communication and action to provide value for all their primary stakeholders (customers, employees, partners, communities, and shareholders). This means that shareholders are only one of many important constituencies. These companies have proven that when culture and social capitalism come first, profit follows.

None of these social capitalistic companies is perfect. They all have difficulties in different areas, which will always occur when you put humans together to work collaboratively; however, what they have in common is more powerful than their differences.

A company must focus on its stakeholders, not just its shareholders. Building a culture that considers and embraces stakeholders also yields greater profit.

These companies understand that they must look at performance from the perspective of all primary stakeholders, not just stockholders. They see society as a whole as a major stakeholder. They create value through connection: emotionally, experientially, socially, and financially. It is the emotional component of the organizational culture that is the "secret sauce" to a successful future for any organization. These companies use emotions as the fuel of their behavioral norms aimed to support society and social capitalism.

The authors of *Firms of Endearment* identify 30 companies that through organizational culture have managed to optimize total stakeholder value instead of focusing strictly on profits. The 30 companies, listed alphabetically, are:

1. Amazon.com (Nasdaq: AMZN)
2. Best Buy (NYSE: BBY)
3. BMW (XETRA – German Stock Exchange)
4. CarMax (NYSE: KMX)
5. Caterpillar (NYSE: CAT)
6. Commerce Bancorp (NYSE: CBH)
7. The Container Store (Privately Held Company)
8. Costco (Nasdaq: COST)
9. eBay (Nasdaq: EBAY)
10. Google (Nasdaq: GOOG)
11. Harley-Davidson (NYSE: HOG)
12. Honda (NYSE: HMC)
13. IDEO (Subsidiary of Steelcase office furniture manufacturer)
14. IKEA (Privately Held Company)
15. JetBlue (Nasdaq: JBLU)

16. Johnson & Johnson (NYSE: JNJ)
17. Jordan's Furniture (Privately Held Company)
18. L.L. Bean (Privately Held Company)
19. New Balance (Privately Held Company)
20. Patagonia (Privately Held Company)
21. Progressive (NYSE: PGR)
22. REI (Privately Held Company)
23. Southwest Airlines (NYSE: LUV)
24. Starbucks (Nasdaq: SBUX)
25. Timberland (NYSE: TBL)
26. Toyota (NYSE: TM)
27. Trader Joe's (Privately Held Company)
28. UPS (NYSE: UPS)
29. Wegmans (Privately Held Company)
30. Whole Foods Market (Nasdaq: WFM)

For this book, I have tracked the long-term stock performance of these aforementioned companies that are publicly traded. The graph on the following page demonstrates the financial performance of five groups of companies over a 10-year period by looking at the average change in stock price since January 1, 2004: (1) "social capitalism" companies; (2) high-performing "classic capitalism" companies; (3) the NASDAQ Composite Index; (4) the S&P 500; and (5) the Dow Jones Industrial Index.

The Dow Jones Industrial Index, the S&P 500, and the NASDAQ are well-known indices that are often used as performance benchmarks. They include organizations in every business sector and frequently serve as indicators of overall economic/market health.

The "classic capitalism" group represents the companies identified by Jim Collins in his famous book, *Good to Great*. He looked at eleven companies that he had identified as moving from "good to great" because they were able to deliver *exceptional returns to investors* over an extended period of time. His criterion was that the companies he identified were able to produce cumulative returns three times greater than the market as a whole (at the time the book was published in 2001).

The "social capitalism" group consists of the 18 publicly held companies that focus on social capitalism, as identified in *Firms of Endearment*; companies that take into consideration cause and complex constituencies, allowing profits to follow these priorities.

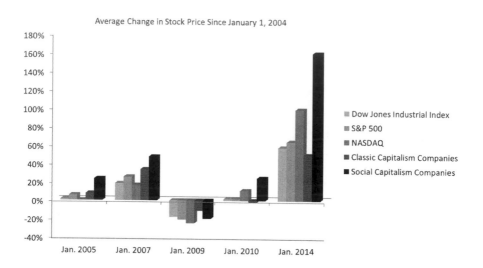

Figure 1. Change in stock price among social capitalism companies, classic capitalism companies, NASDAQ, S&P 500, and Dow Jones Industrial Index.

What is immediately apparent from the graph is that social capitalism companies are wildly outperforming all other groups of companies – even the "best of the best" companies identified in *Good to Great*. Also important to note is that this performance advantage begins at the one-year mark: an impressive 24% return for social capitalism companies versus anywhere from a low of 0% (NASDAQ) to a max of 8% (classic capitalism companies). And by the time we get to the ten-year mark, the gap between social capitalism companies and everyone else has widened to almost absurd proportions: a whopping 160% return for social capitalism companies versus a low of 50% (for classic capitalism companies) to a high of 99% (NASDAQ) for the indices. So that persistent belief that "doing good takes a long time to deliver financial returns"? Patently, demonstrably false. Social capitalism does *good* (makes the world a better place) and does *better* (delivers higher returns to shareholders) from the beginning – and the performance gap just gets bigger and bigger with time.

Companies that focus on social capitalism not only offer greater returns to their shareholders, but they do so by prioritizing the needs of their complex constituencies and allowing profits to follow. For example, customers who shop at Whole Foods pay a premium for eggs that they would not have to pay at a discount grocery, but they are willing to pay that premium for the emotional experience accompanied with "doing the right thing" by purchasing eggs produced by free-range hens. It is the Whole Foods Whole Trade brand that represents social capitalism through its requirements of: (1) a fair price for crops; (2) environmentally sound and sustainable practices; (3) better wages and labor conditions; and (4) premium-quality products. This is how Whole Foods, through its Whole Trade brand, takes into account its complex constituencies (stakeholders).

Employees are also important stakeholders. Costco, on average, pays its employees 65% more than Wal-Mart and 40% more than Sam's Club. It also offers employees a more generous benefits package. Interestingly, with these higher expenses, Costco also generates substantially more profit per employee than Sam's Club. These profits are realized by creating greater efficiency. Costco spends only 9.7% of its earnings on sales, general and administrative expenses (SG&A); it is more than 20% for both Sam's Club and Wal-Mart. Costco's employee turnover is also very low; 6% in year one, compared with 21% at Sam's Club and 50% at Wal-Mart. [5,6]

When companies build cultures that value stakeholders (society as a whole, customers, employees, etc.) and value the connections between these constituencies, expenses decrease, profits increase, and everybody wins.

Results Matter

Given this data, why don't more companies adopt this focus on a culture that recognizes interdependent constituencies? When profit is the primary driver, Wall Street is your primary constituent. Wall Street looks for performance on a quarterly, rather than long-term, basis. It is this type of pressure that makes many CEOs sacrifice long-term investments to make their short-term quarterly numbers look more favorable. This may produce short-term profit for a period of time. But, eventually, when long-term investments are sacrificed for quarterly earnings reports, short-term investors (including the CEO, through enormous compensation plans and golden parachutes) are the only constituencies that win ... at everyone else's expense.

 Companies that focus on culture create value for all their stakeholders and offer exceptional stock market returns in both the near and long term, in addition to building long-term loyalty from employees, customers, vendors, and investors.

So What?

Profit comes as a result of human connections. These connections are made, in part, through social proof. Companies can invest an inordinate amount of resources preparing ethics manuals and values guidelines, but in the end, it is the behaviors displayed by their leaders that will provide social proof as to what are desirable and undesirable behaviors.

Cause is also a factor that fuels human connection and drives human behavior. Throughout this chapter, there have been several examples of entrepreneurs and companies that effectively use cause to connect with all of their stakeholders.

The consumer-driven, zero-sum game, materialistic society is shifting to a society focused on experiencing connections between beings. This connection comes from an organizational culture that focuses on how each company interacts with its stakeholders, not just stockholders.

As a business model, social capitalism has shown great success, long-term viability, and profitability. The greatest advantage of this model is that it delivers outstanding results for all of its stakeholders, including owners, shareholders, employees, customers, vendors, partners, and entire communities.

Taking Action

1. Where do you see the biggest disconnects between what is said or written (policies) and what is done (behaviors, social proof) in your organization?
2. How would you define your organization's cause? How would your employees define it?
3. What percentage of behavior in your organization is driven by profit? What percentage is driven by cause?
4. What can you do to encourage your company to broaden its consideration beyond just shareholders to all stakeholders?

CHAPTER 4

HABIT PATTERNS

"All of our life, so far as it has form, is but a mass of habits."

– William James,
Philosopher and Psychologist

What You Need To Know:

1. Our behavior is largely a bundle of habit patterns.

2. Every habit pattern, no matter how simple or complex, is malleable.

3. Mental habit patterns hang together because of a process called "chunking."

4. Behavioral habit patterns hang together because of a process called "chaining."

5. Strong cultures create and demand behaviors that, when repeated, become habit patterns that occur automatically and without thought.

6. When a habit pattern is established, brain effort goes down, allowing the brain to focus on other things.

7. Every habit pattern has three pieces: cue, routine, and reward.

8. Cravings drive habit patterns.

9. The Platinum Rule of Habit Pattern Shift: you can change a habit pattern by keeping the same cue and reward and simply changing the routine.

10. Data shows that top CEOs consistently display habit patterns involving integrity, responsibility, forgiveness, and compassion.

11. Ultimately, CEOs get the cultures (and the companies) they deserve because they are responsible for creating them.

Habits do not exist in a vacuum. They are part of a complex set of behaviors referred to as habit patterns. Your brain would shut down without habit patterns. It simply could not manage the various stimuli it takes in every second of the day. Habit patterns are part of what allow us to function in the world. Nonetheless, habit patterns are not our destiny; they can be ignored, changed, and replaced.

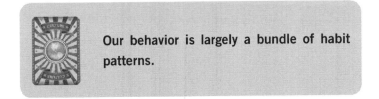

Our behavior is largely a bundle of habit patterns.

What was the first thing you did when you woke up this morning? Did you grab your cell phone or tablet to check your email or the morning news? Did you jump into the shower? Did you brush your teeth before or after breakfast? Most of these decisions and others we make during the course of a day may feel like well-thought-out, independent choices, but they're not. They're habit patterns; patterns that make much of our behavior predictable and routine. In fact, a paper published in 2006 by Bas Verplanken and Wendy Wood found that more than 40% of the behaviors people exhibit on any given day do not come from decisions, but from habit patterns.[1]

Habit patterns have a tremendous influence on what we eat, if or when we exercise, when we pay our bills, how we work, how we respond to others, and if we maintain our health and happiness. For every habit that we have, at some point in the past, we made a decision regarding how to handle each of these potential situations. Soon after, we stopped making choices and the behaviors became part of our habit patterns.

> **Every habit pattern, no matter how simple or complex, is malleable.**

It is important to understand that every habit pattern, no matter how simple or complex, no matter whether it is our own or someone else's, is malleable. A leader must understand that to change one's own habit pattern, it takes work in the form of time, dedication, and mindfulness.

Strong cultures create and demand specific habit patterns from their members. To new members in the culture, the behaviors may be unfamiliar, and they require thought and effort. But over time, these new behaviors will become established as old behaviors, becoming part of a habit pattern, and happening automatically.

The Biology Behind Habit Patterns

> **Mental habit patterns hang together because of a process called "chunking."**

Neurologically, the process by which the brain converts a sequence of neural firing events into a routine or habit pattern is referred to as "chunking." When a series of neurons fire in a sequence or pattern repeatedly, that sequence or pattern of firing gets "tied" together through chunking.

Behavioral habit patterns hang together because of a process called "chaining."

In the realm of human behavior, this type of sequencing is called "chaining." When a series of movements or behaviors are repeated in a particular sequence, they are "tied" together through an association called chaining. In essence, the repetition of a behavioral pattern creates a chain reaction. Once the first behavior occurs, the remaining behaviors almost inevitably follow.

Cognitive chunking and behavioral chaining occur because, as an organism, humans are always looking for ways to conserve energy and effort. Without our own intervention, our brains will always try to convert any repeated routine into a habit pattern, simply because it allows the brain to expend less energy by ramping down more often. Evolutionarily, this was a huge advantage. An efficient brain that doesn't have to focus on habit patterns such as walking and eating can devote more energy to other thoughts, such as inventing spears for hunting, and more recently, airplanes and video games.

Strong cultures create and demand behaviors that, when repeated, become habit patterns that occur automatically and without thought.

In a strong organizational culture, habit patterns are formed through social proof rather than policies. Strong cultures demand certain habit patterns from their members such as connectedness, integrity to develop trust, belonging, and group membership. In a strong culture, these are behaviors group members don't need to "think" about displaying. They occur naturally without prompt or thought because they are part of the cultural behavioral norm and/or habit pattern. These habit patterns can be traced back to a specific part of the brain called the basal ganglia.

The Role of the Basal Ganglia

In the center of our brain is a golf ball-sized bundle of tissue, similar to the structure found inside the brains of fish, reptiles, birds, and other mammals. This bundle of tissue is called the basal ganglia. For years, scientists weren't quite sure what it did or what it was responsible for other than knowing that, when it malfunctioned, diseases such as Parkinson's would develop.

The Brain and Cognitive Sciences Department of the Massachusetts Institute of Technology (MIT) is the epicenter of the revolution that has been taking place in the science of habit pattern formation. It is there, through rat and other animal studies, that science has learned what is happening in our brains when we do mundane tasks such as wash our hands, brush our teeth, or drive to work.

In the mid 1990s, researchers at MIT began to observe that animals that had injured basal ganglia had difficulty performing tasks they had previously performed, such as manipulating containers to obtain food or run through mazes.[2] Using state-of-the-art technology, the researchers connected electrodes to the brains of healthy rats and observed what was going on in their brains as the animals performed different routines. Eventually, the animals were put into a T-shaped maze with a piece of chocolate as the reward.

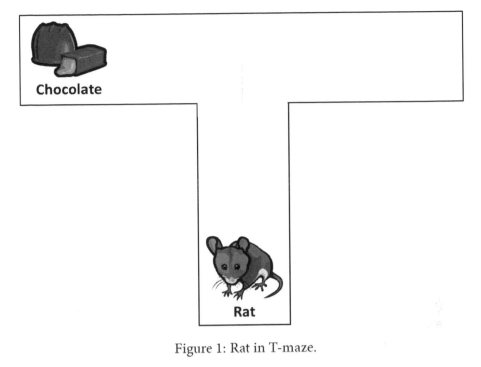

Figure 1: Rat in T-maze.

The experiment was set up so that the rat was placed at the bottom of the T, with a partition between it and the rest of the maze, and the reward for all trials was always placed at the end of the top left portion of the maze. The experimenter would start the trial by making a loud click sound and opening the partition. Behaviorally, what the experimenters observed was the rat wandering up and down the vertical part of the T, sniffing in the corners and scratching the walls. It appeared the rat could smell the chocolate, but wasn't sure how to find it. Very often, when the rat reached the top of the T, it would turn right, away from the chocolate, go to the end of the right top section of the T, then turn around and make its way back to the top left section of the T, where it would find its reward. Eventually, most animals found the reward, but behaviorally, there was no discernible pattern to how it went about doing so.

Neurologically, the picture was very different. While each rat was initially making its way through the maze, its brain – in particular, its basal ganglia – fired furiously. The electrodes showed that each time the rat would scratch a wall or sniff the air for the smell of chocolate, the brain increased its activity, trying to make meaning of the scents, sights, and sounds. While the behavior seemed casual, the function of the brain was purposeful.

 When a habit pattern is established, brain effort goes down, allowing the brain to focus on other things.

The researchers repeated the experiments multiple times and monitored the rats' brains as they moved through the maze. As they did, a series of shifts became evident. Behaviorally, the rats stopped sniffing at the corners, scratching the walls, and making wrong turns; they would simply get to the reward faster and faster. This was not a surprise; they had clearly learned. The surprise came neurologically. As each rat learned to go through the maze faster and faster, the brain activity actually *decreased*. As the activity became more automatic (habit pattern formation) the rats processed information ("thought") less and less. As the habit pattern of running the maze strengthened, the brain activity of processing information from scratching and sniffing decreased. The rat didn't need to "make a decision" about which direction to turn at the top of the T, so the decision-making centers in its brain were quiet. Running the maze had become a habit pattern for the rat, so it did not need to activate the decision-making part of its brain.

This habit pattern formation relied upon activity that occurred in the basal ganglia. This was the part of the brain that continued its activity as the rest of the brain quieted down. As the rat ran the maze faster and faster, most of its brain worked less and less. It was the basal ganglia that stored and utilized the habit patterns while the rest of the brain went quiet.

Behavioral economist, Princeton University professor, Nobel Prize Laureate, and author of *Thinking, Fast and Slow*,[3] Daniel Kahneman, describes this phenomenon in human decision making as humans having two systems of thought:

- *System 1* is an "automatic," intuitive-based system that he summarizes as fast thinking. I would call this relying on a well-formed habit pattern or a response based on a strong habit pattern.
- *System 2* is an "effortful," thoughtful system, which he refers to as slow thinking, in that it requires time, effort, and thought. I would call this mindfulness or conscious decision making.

A quick example: what is 2 + 2? The answer that comes to mind is part of System 1, a fast, automatic part of a habit pattern learned through repetition. You can produce the response without a moment's thought. What is 13 x 27? This response would come from System 2. You can calculate the answer, but it would take some effort and thought. It is not part of an established habit pattern. Responses from System 1 come from complex habit patterns. Responses from System 2 come from more thoughtful, considered thinking.

Behavioral Development of Habit Patterns

So how is it that we can move from System 2, a set of thoughts or behaviors that require our focus and attention, to System 1, a set of thoughts and behaviors that can occur more automatically? The answer lies in the understanding of the components of habit patterns: the cue, the routine, and the reward.

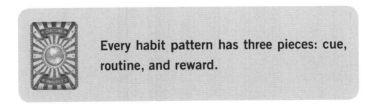

Every habit pattern has three pieces: cue, routine, and reward.

There are two distinct ways of developing habit patterns: (1) the development of new habit patterns from scratch and (2) the changing of existing habit patterns. With regard to the first, there are three steps to creating a habit pattern from scratch. First is the cue. A cue is a trigger that instructs the brain to go into automatic mode and activate a particular habit pattern. Second is the routine. A routine can be a set of mental steps, physical behaviors, or emotional responses that are required to make it to the third step, the reward. A reward helps our brains determine whether the routine is worth remembering as a habit pattern for the future. Over time, these steps – cue, routine, and reward – become the habit pattern in the basal ganglia that allows our brains to focus on other things as we execute the habit pattern, each time becoming more automatic. Eventually, the cue and the reward become associated in the brain, creating a sense of craving when the cue is present. It is this craving (emotion) that fuels the habit pattern.

This pattern can be clearly seen in the development of new romantic relationships. The cue is the person to whom you are romantically attracted. The routine becomes all the things you do together as a budding couple to enjoy each other's company. The reward – well – you get the picture. Very quickly, the brain makes a powerful connection between the cue (your romantic partner) and the reward, to the point where just the sight of your romantic partner will create a physical and emotional craving.

This science leads us to a basic truth about habit patterns: when you are behaving on the basis of a habit pattern (System 1), the brain is not fully participating in decision making. Habit patterns are what allow your brain to conserve energy, as it is working less hard, which enables it to focus on other tasks. People often describe their System 1 responses as feeling "automatic." Think about people in our world that are "perched and ready to leap," meaning they are always prepared to jump into a conflict or confrontation. They often describe their behavior as automatic or unstoppable. Therefore, unless you deliberately fight against a habit pattern you do not want to exhibit, unless you find new routines as part of the habit pattern, the habit pattern will be executed automatically in a way that feels out of your control. However, understanding what drives habit patterns allows us to develop and shape them, in ourselves and in others.

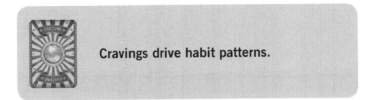

Cravings drive habit patterns.

Craving brains fuel habit pattern creation. Cravings occur when there is a strong association between a cue, which triggers a new habit pattern, and the reward that follows. When the cue is present, the craving arises, driving the habit pattern behavior in order to achieve the reward.

Cravings occur naturally when there is a strong association between the cue and the reward. When the cue is present, the reward is desired (craved), and the habit pattern is automatically exhibited to achieve the reward and fulfill the craving.

This is how strong cultures are formed. Members of the culture crave a reward (for example, connectedness, belonging, a cause larger than themselves, or giving back to society) because the culture teaches its members that these things are important and rewards its members for the routines supporting the culture. There is a cue (for example, a task, an initiative, or a special project) that is tied to a routine (a set of behaviors or processes). With repetition, the cue and the reward become strongly associated with each other, so when the cue is present, members in the culture crave the reward.

The understanding (and exploitation) of habit patterns goes back at least 100 years. It has been used in a variety of ways to change the behavior of millions of people. From manufacturing to marketing, we have seen that understanding how to change habit patterns is a powerful force to change behavior, even in large groups of people.

Jonesing for Pepsodent

In the early 1900s, Claude C. Hopkins became part of the team that would make a new toothpaste a household name: "Pepsodent." He was already wealthy from work he had done to make other previously unknown products common in American households. Some of these products included Quaker Oats, Bissell carpet sweepers, and Goodyear tires.

At the time, as the nation became wealthier and began to consume larger amounts of processed and sugary foods it had not consumed previously, the health of American's teeth was in a steady and steep decline. When America entered into World War I, military officials found so many recruits had rotting teeth that they identified dental hygiene as a national security risk.

Part of the problem came from the types of food that were being consumed. The other part of the problem came from that fact that, at the time, almost no one brushed their teeth. Before Pepsodent came on the market, only 7% of Americans had a tube of toothpaste in their household. Ten years after Hopkins' national advertising campaign, 65% of Americans had toothpaste in their homes.

At the beginning of his advertising campaign, Hopkins was already well-schooled in the psychology of habit pattern formation and the need to find a cue (a trigger to initiate a new behavior), a routine (tooth brushing using Pepsodent), and a reward that would be associated with the cue that would later create a craving. To drive this radical change in dental hygiene, Hopkins identified a cue (trigger) that he believed would change behavior. In dental textbooks, he found several references to mucin plaques, which in his advertising campaign he called a 'film.' The presence of this film could be easily identified by running your tongue across the front of your teeth, which people apparently did readily upon simple suggestion, and as you might have just done yourself.

The reward, as Hopkins portrayed it, was the achievement of beauty. Soon after the initiation of the campaign, cities all over the country were plastered with Pepsodent advertisements with beautiful people smiling and exclaiming, "Note how many pretty teeth are seen everywhere." "Millions are using a new method of teeth cleansing. Why would any woman have dingy film on her teeth? Pepsodent removes the film!"

But beauty was not the only craving that the new behavior created. Pepsodent was the only toothpaste of its time to use both citric acids and mint oil. These served as mild irritants to the gums and tongue, which users experienced as a tingling sensation when they used Pepsodent. When they didn't use Pepsodent, they craved the tingling sensation, establishing a physical craving, beyond beauty, and a vivid reminder that they had not brushed their teeth. Users of Pepsodent craved beauty, and *learned* to crave (habit pattern formation) the tingling sensation brought on by the citric acids and mint oils.

Within three weeks of the initiation of the advertisement campaign, Pepsodent couldn't keep up with demand. Within ten years, Pepsodent was one of the most popular brands in the world, and remained America's best-selling toothpaste for more than thirty years, which is how long it took for competing toothpastes to break the strong habit pattern created by Pepsodent's original habit pattern shift.

All this could not have been possible if Hopkins did not understand the formation of habit patterns and the application of the "platinum rule" of habit pattern shift.

Having established the rules for creating new habit patterns from scratch, the next challenge is to create changes in existing habit patterns. This type of shift, in ourselves or in others, is achieved through the application of the "Platinum Rule of Habit Pattern Shift."

 The Platinum Rule of Habit Pattern Shift: you can change a habit pattern by keeping the same cue and reward and simply changing the routine.

I refer to it as the Platinum Rule of Habit Pattern Shift because in business, we can't always change the cue or increase the reward. If our culture has already established a cause in which you "change the world and/or change human experience in the world," and that cause is the reward for the current routines that make your business successful, you won't want to change the cause/reward. However, if a business factor (such as the economy) shifts, you may have to shift the routine of your teams without shifting the cue or the reward. The Platinum Rule of Habit Pattern Shift instructs us on how to do that. While keeping the cue and reward the same, we can change the routine.

The evidence for this is all in. If you want to create a shift in habit patterns, you must first understand the cue, the routine, and the reward – and the relationship between these three components. The mechanism behind this shift comes from the strong association between the cue and reward. This association drives a craving that is satisfied by achieving the reward that can only be reached through a particular routine. Because of some need or desire, through behavioral rehearsal or practice, the routine can be changed after the cue is presented, with assurance that the reward will be the same or greater. For people to be willing to change their routine (risk losing the reward), they must believe (trust) that change is possible and the reward will be the same or greater. People tend to be willing to take risks and trust if they are part of a group (connectedness, belonging) that is doing so with them or has already done so.

In smoking cessation programs, participants are first encouraged to change their routines to diminish cravings and find a support group of others trying to quit smoking or a collection of former smokers who have already successfully quit. The support group helps establish the belief that the smoker can also quit and helps the smoker when he or she begins to fear relapse.

The same strategy has been applied to weight loss. For people who want to lose weight, they need to learn the trigger that sets off their routine of eating and overeating, find someone who can help them change their routine when they experience a craving (have a conversation or go for a walk), and others who have successfully lost weight.

The Platinum Rule of Habit Pattern Shift in Action

Tony Dungy was head coach of the Tampa Bay Buccaneers from 1996 to 2001, and head coach of the Indianapolis Colts from 2002 to 2008. Dungy became the first African American head coach to win the Super Bowl when his Colts defeated the Chicago Bears in Super Bowl XLI. Dungy set a new NFL record for consecutive playoff appearances by a head coach in 2008 after securing his tenth straight playoff appearance after a win against the Jacksonville Jaguars. He achieved all this success because he knew and applied the Platinum Rule of Habit Pattern Shift.

Dungy had a very specific coaching philosophy that he believed would create a winning team. He articulated this as: "Champions don't do extraordinary things. They do ordinary things, but they do them without thinking, too fast for the other team to react. They follow the habits they've learned."

Dungy understood that you could never truly erase an old habit. He also understood that habit patterns are part of a three-step process: cue, routine, and reward. His approach was simply to attack the middle step: routine. He understood that to shift a habit pattern you must keep the existing cue, continue the existing reward, and replace the routine. This was the formula that Dungy applied throughout his career as head coach to ensure his teams performed using habit patterns rather than having to make decisions on the field.

There were several other things that Dungy understood and applied. He understood that players must believe that change was possible, that they would receive the same or increased rewards, and that they would receive support from others around them to achieve the necessary changes.

Understanding how to change habit patterns is critical to creating a shift in culture. A culture provides both direction and support for the change in behavior, increasing the success of behavior change.

Habit Pattern Shift Inside Organizations: Focus on the Fundamentals

Certain habit patterns are more important to change than others. These are referred to as fundamental habit patterns. Fundamental habit patterns refer to behaviors that are strongly linked with other behaviors and create behavioral chain reactions. By changing one part of a habit pattern, other habit patterns must also change. This chain reaction occurs throughout an organization. Some habit patterns are more important in our lives because they have greater influence on other habit patterns. These are the ones that are fundamental. Over time, these habit patterns have the potential to transform how people behave at work, at play, and at home. It is these fundamental habit patterns that serve as levers to shift and reshape other habit patterns.

If, as an individual, a family member, or a leader of an organization, you focus your energies on changing fundamental habit patterns, you can create shifts in other important behaviors and behavior norms. Positive and healthy fundamental habit patterns help create new habit patterns and become part of a flourishing new culture.

Researchers have found fundamental habit patterns in virtually every organization they have studied. And, of course, some of these fundamental habit patterns are more desirable than others. Alcoa serves as an excellent example of fundamental habit pattern shift from problematic ones to more positive (and ultimately more profitable) ones. They were once a traditional aluminum manufacturer that faced challenges in productivity and profitability. Focusing on a single fundamental habit pattern changed the entire organization.

Fundamental Habit Patterns and Alcoa

The Aluminum Company of America was founded in 1907. In 1910, it became known as Alcoa, taking the acronym as its official name in 1999. Like many organizations that are more than 100 years old, Alcoa has seen good times and bad. One of its more difficult times came in 1987. Alcoa's management had led it as an organization in a series of missteps. In essence, it had tried to expand into a series of new product lines without securing its ability to maintain its current customers. As a result, Alcoa found itself losing customers to competitors, and profits dwindled.

Investors in the company seemed relieved when Alcoa's board announced it would be changing its leadership. That relief was short-lived when it was announced the new CEO would be Paul O'Neill. O'Neill was known by few people in the investor community, and those who did know of him, only knew him as a former government bureaucrat. What was a brief sense of relief turned into panic when O'Neill first spoke to investors.

O'Neill told investors, "If you want to understand how Alcoa is doing, you need to look at our workplace safety figures. If we bring our injury rates down, it won't be because of cheerleading or nonsense you sometimes hear from other CEOs, it will be because the individuals at this company have agreed to become part of something important. They've devoted themselves to creating a habit of excellence. Safety will be an indicator that we're making progress in changing our habits across the entire institution. That's how we should be judged."[4]

Investors left the room shocked and dismayed. Many told their clients to sell their stock immediately, before others began to do the same. It was the worst piece of advice they could have given their clients.

Less than one year after O'Neill's introductory speech, Alcoa hit record high profits. When O'Neill retired in 2000, Alcoa's net income was five times greater than before he had arrived, and its market capitalization had risen by $27 billion. An investor who had invested $1 million in Alcoa on the day O'Neill became CEO would have earned $1 million in dividends, and the value of their stock would have quintupled.[5]

O'Neill took a notoriously dangerous, large, stodgy company and turned it into a model of profit and safety by doing one thing: focusing on fundamental habit patterns.

Alcoa: Habit Pattern Shift Leads to Success

At the time O'Neill took over, critics had broadly lambasted Alcoa for the inflexibility of its workforce and the poor quality of its product. It is well known that at a company as large and established as Alcoa, a new CEO couldn't come in and simply demand everyone work harder and be more productive in order to improve efficiency and quality. The previous CEO had tried to mandate improvements – and found himself with 15,000 employees on strike. At the time, it was described by some as being "far from a happy family – more like the Manson family with access to molten metal."[6]

With all these issues, O'Neill did not make profitability, efficiency, or quality his top priority. He knew he would have to focus on an issue that everyone – management, unions, and employees – could agree upon. He would choose a habit pattern that would bring people together with little or no resistance, and he would leverage this habit pattern to create change.

O'Neill decided that the fundamental habit pattern to focus on would be safety. He had a strong belief that everyone who worked for Alcoa had the right to leave work in the same condition in which they entered. He believed Alcoa employees should not have to risk their lives in order to feed their families.

O'Neill set an audacious safety goal: zero injuries. That would be his commitment, no matter the cost. O'Neill already knew that profit would be a result of efficient and effective performance, and balancing Alcoa's stakeholders. He saw clearly that his employees were indeed stakeholders. So, he focused on the fundamental habit patterns that would improve performance through employee safety, knowing profits would follow.

Part of O'Neill's brilliance came from his realization that no one would fight him on the safety issue. Unions wouldn't fight him because they had been fighting for worker safety rules for years. Managers wouldn't fight him because injuries lowered productivity and morale.

O'Neill's safety plan would radically change habit patterns throughout Alcoa. Alcoa had to become the safest aluminum company on the planet. He did this by again applying the Platinum Rule for Habit Pattern Shift.

He first identified the cue: an employee injury. He then instituted a new routine: any incident in which an employee was injured required the unit president to contact him within 24 hours with a report of the incident, its cause, and a plan that would ensure the injury would never recur. The reward: those who embraced the system would be promoted.

As these fundamental safety habit patterns shifted, other habit patterns began to shift as well. For years, the unions had resisted any type of performance measurement on individual employees. With safety being the focus, this individual measurement system was embraced because it made everyone aware when a manufacturing process was getting sideways and risking safety. Managers had previously resisted policies offering employees the autonomy to slow or shut down a production line because the pace was too accelerated. When safety was the focus, this was embraced because it was a quick way to prevent injuries.

As O'Neill's approach moved through the organization, costs went down, quality went up, and productivity peaked.[7] If molten metal was injuring employees because it splashed, the pouring system would be redesigned, which would lead to fewer injuries. This also had the benefit of saving money because less raw material would be lost in the manufacturing process. If a machine had a history of breaking down, it would be replaced, posing less risk of injury to the employee working that machine or to the employee who had to fix it. This also had the benefit of producing a higher-quality product. Alcoa quickly learned that equipment malfunctions were a significant cause of poor quality aluminum.

At Alcoa, O'Neill's approach to establishing new habit patterns created a new culture: one in which the safety of workers came first, and profits naturally followed. Alcoa was an example of how changes to a specific habit pattern can solve a specific challenge. There are, however, a set of universal habit patterns that are critical for success for all organizations, regardless of the specific challenges those organizations face.

Fundamental Habit Patterns of CEOs that Lead to Organizational Success

At this point, certain names are familiar to us all. Bernie Ebbers (WorldCom), Bernie Madoff (the largest fraud in U.S. history), Jeffery Skilling (Enron), Rajat Gupta (insider trading). All these infamous names have one thing in common: they were all convicted of white-collar crimes that harmed society and its individuals, both financially and emotionally.

Most white-collar criminals have a habit pattern problem. Part of their problem is that they don't understand the formation of habit patterns. They begin with an initial behavior, which they most likely have to think about and consider before doing. That behavior is likely in a "grey area," on the border between legal and illegal. Because it is the first time that behavior is executed, it is likely small enough that they do not get caught. As a result, they receive a (usually) substantial reward without penalty. This reward serves to reinforce the behavior. Soon after, the pattern of behavior is repeated (cue, routine, reward) ... and expanded. Eventually, the behavior becomes automatic, without thought, thereby becoming a habit pattern.

Any behavior that goes uncorrected and has a strong reward can easily become a habit pattern, whether that behavior is legal or illegal, or considered right or wrong. Similarly, no one ever (initially) intends to violate his or her code of ethics. Ethics violations generally begin with a little behavior that is a baby step across an ethical line. If that behavior is rewarded, it will quickly become a habit pattern, which can ultimately lead to an individual's downfall.

Many believe that these types of illegal behaviors are a result of character. I would suggest what others call character or personality is nothing more than a bundle of habit patterns (cue, routine, reward). Ann Graybiel, the MIT scientist who was responsible for many of the basal ganglia experiments, states, "Habits never really disappear. They're encoded into the structure of a brain. The problem is that a brain can't tell the difference between bad and good habits, and so if you have a bad one, it's always lurking there, waiting for the right cues and reward."[8]

This is part of why, in the field of drug treatment, addicts are always told that they must "change people, places, and things." This is because people, places, and things form strong cues for well-ingrained routines, which lead to the craving for drugs. Yet, even drug addicts can stay clean by understanding – and more importantly, *behaving* – differently. This means changing habit patterns.

In 2007, Doug Lennick and Fred Kiel published a book called *Moral Intelligence*, which suggested that a leader's character can determine an organization's financial performance.[9] They received some pushback against that premise from the business community, which believed that things like moral character are a "nice thing to have," but that the business plan is really what determines the success of a business.

As a result, Lennick and Kiel began to collect data on 100 CEOs in a national research study. Their aim was to collect hard evidence to see if a leader's character and personality (bundle of habit patterns) affected the financial performance of an organization.

They defined character in a specific manner: character is something that can be inferred through observable behavior. It is seen in how a leader treats others when they have nothing to gain from the interaction or "when no one else is looking."

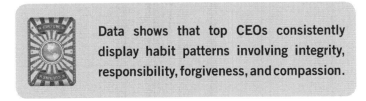

Data shows that top CEOs consistently display habit patterns involving integrity, responsibility, forgiveness, and compassion.

The researchers were able to rate a CEO's character by developing an instrument that looked at the CEO on four characteristics and had the employees rate the CEO on each of these. The four "moral principles" (Lennick and Kiel's term) that the survey found defined a high-character CEO were:

- *Integrity*: acting consistently with the principles, values, and beliefs one professes (walking the walk), telling the truth, standing up for what is right, and keeping promises
- *Responsibility*: taking responsibility for personal choices, admitting mistakes and failures, embracing responsibility for serving others; "being a steward" of the organization and its resources
- *Forgiveness*: demonstrating the ability to let go of one's mistakes and let go of other's mistakes
- *Compassion*: empathy without judgment

Once Lennick and Kiel looked at their CEOs on these measures of character, they ranked the CEOs based on their character scores and divided the whole group at the median to see if there would be a difference in performance between upper half and low lower half CEOs. They used return on assets (ROA) and employee engagement as business metrics.

The results were astonishing. For CEOs below the median, their ROA was 1.9%. For CEOs above the median, their ROA was 5.3%. That is an almost threefold difference. When they removed the average performers on their measure of character (Integrity, Responsibility, Forgiveness, and Compassion) and looked at the high character versus low character CEOs, the results were even more pronounced. The high character CEOs had an ROA of 8.39%; the low character CEOs had an ROA of -0.57%. The low character CEOs were actually diminishing the value of the company for investors. Their results for employee engagement showed similar patterns.

Although the results of their study seem conclusive, I would suggest their use of character is problematic. As I said earlier, character is a bundle of habit patterns. The problem is that character, like personality, is often seen as a stable, static trait, rather than a state that is influenced by environment. Culture trumps everything – including biology and psychology, of which personality and character are a part. Lennick and Kiel even state that character can be changed, just as habit patterns can certainly be changed. People change habit patterns all the time. It is simply much easier to do so when they understand the structure of habit patterns and how they are formed.

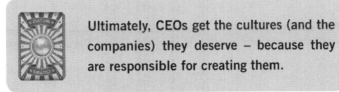

Ultimately, CEOs get the cultures (and the companies) they deserve – because they are responsible for creating them.

The challenge for CEOs is that they create the environment for everyone that works with and for them. They are responsible for creating the cues and rewards that drive the routines that tie employees together. They are responsible for the culture that surrounds them. Ultimately, CEOs get the culture they create and cultivate.

So What?

It is important to understand that behaviors don't exist in a vacuum. They occur in a context, environment, or culture. Habits are nothing more than a group of behaviors that hang together. Habit patterns are a sequence of habits that are tied together through chunking and chaining, initiated by a cue that triggers the routine, which is then followed by a reward. Once a habit pattern is established, it cannot be erased; it is hardwired into the brain. However, habit patterns *can* be changed.

Every habit pattern, no matter how simple or complex, is malleable. A leader must understand that to change one's own habit patterns takes work in the form of time, dedication, and mindfulness. If you can understand your own cues, routines, and rewards and how they come together, you can change your own habit patterns – and those of others – hopefully for the better.

Taking Action

1. What are some individual habit patterns of your own that you would like to change?

2. As a leader, what are some of the fundamental habit patterns you would like to develop for yourself?

3. Within your organization, what are some of the habit patterns among employees that need to shift in order to ensure greater success?

4. Within your organization, what new fundamental habit patterns could change your organizational culture and performance?

CHAPTER 5

CONNECTEDNESS

"No one cares how much you know, until
they know how much you care."

– Theodore Roosevelt,
26th President of the United States

What You Need To Know:

1. Connectedness has evolved over thousands of years and exists in humans and other mammals.

2. Connectedness is a function of both biology and psychology.

3. Human beings' primary drives are to experience connectedness and belonging.

4. If we want to build institutions, societies, or cultures that involve connectedness and belonging, we must be willing to discuss the *actual* primary drivers of human behavior.

5. Self-interest, violence, and aggression are secondary drives that arise when our primary drives are stifled in some way.

6. Connectedness is the open display of enthusiasm, affection, or kindness – and it requires warmth. Warmth trumps competence.

7. People perceived as warm develop greater trust, connectedness, and belonging with those around them.

8. Organizations that lack warmth and connectedness often have a culture of "everyone for themselves."

9. Warmth in organizations leads to greater profit.

In the late 1990s, there was a study done in Parma, Italy.[1] Scientists had a macaque monkey connected to an MRI machine, while the monkey was trying to open a nut. Their goal was to determine which neurons were firing as the monkey engaged in this simple behavior.

Connectedness has evolved over thousands of years and exists in humans and other mammals.

While this was going on, suddenly and without planning, a human walked into the lab. The person was hungry and saw a bowl of nuts on the table. This individual walked over to the bowl of nuts and started eating them. This was a surprise to the monkey. He was probably thinking something like, who is the stranger coming in and eating my food? The monkey didn't move; he just watched as the human ate the nut, just as he (the monkey) had done moments earlier. The scientists continued to watch the MRI machine, and what they saw surprised them. They saw that the same exact neurons were firing as when the monkey itself had eaten the nuts.

At first, the scientists had no idea as to what was going on. They thought the MRI machine was broken. Then they began to put MRI scanners on other primates, particularly chimpanzees, who also have a big neocortex. Then, they did the same test on humans. What they found with great consistency is the presence of a specific type of neuron called "mirror neurons." All humans are soft-wired with these mirror neurons, and since then, science has found the same is true of most primates, dolphins, and dogs. They all have mirror neurons.

When you observe another's experience, your mirror neurons allow you to share their anger, joy, sadness, frustration, or anxiety. The same neurons firing in their brain are firing in your brain. This is part of what connects us to each other and similar animals, fundamentally, on a biological level.

Mirror neurons form the fundamental biological element of connectedness. What we feel as the psychological experience of emotion, our own and that of others, is rooted in biology.

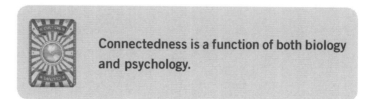

Connectedness is a function of both biology and psychology.

Connectedness can be defined as the ability to understand and share the feelings of another. This is not only about psychology. This is about biology. Connectedness is considered one of the two pillars of morality. Research on morality identifies: (1) reciprocity (fairness) and (2) empathy (compassion/connectedness) as fundamental to human morality.[2] Human morality can be considered to include more than these two, but if you remove these two, the construct collapses. Morality, which is often seen (incorrectly) as exclusively a human attribute, comes from the ability to have and show empathy. It is not a cognitive process and does not require cognition. It has a biological, not psychological, origin.

Whether you are human or a non-human primate, relationships have value. If a particular relationship with value is damaged by conflict, something needs to be done to salvage the relationship. This is true for all of us, both personally (in our home lives) and professionally (in our relationships at work).

Dr. Frans de Waal has been studying reciprocity and empathy in primates for more than thirty years. His findings are quite illuminating.[3] Chimpanzees are known as being power hungry, aggressive, and competitive. Yet, chimpanzees do "make up" after they have fights. If power, dominance, and winning are all that matters, then why would chimpanzees make up after a fight? Because relationships have value and are more important than power, dominance, and winning.

These behaviors are clearly shown in different experiments done by de Waal and his colleagues at the Yerkes center.[4]

Experiment 1: Two chimps, each in its own cage, are placed in front of a box with food in it. The box is too heavy for either chimp to pull towards himself alone. The chimps pull on ropes simultaneously to bring the box closer to them. The chimps coordinate their pulling so they both pull together. Then, they both can get the food.

Experiment 2: The set up in this experiment is the same as Experiment 1. The difference is that in this experiment, one of the chimps has been fed, so he is no longer really interested in the task or the reward (food). In this experiment, the hungry chimp has a complete understanding that he can't do it alone. He needs the cooperation of the other chimp. The chimp that has been fed is not interested, but when he is prompted by the hungry chimp, he still helps to pull the box. The well-fed chimp is still willing to work even though he's not interested in the food because in chimp social groups, when one chimp does a favor for another, it is understood that the favor will be returned in the future.

Experiment 2 is an example of reciprocity. In recent years there has been considerable evidence in research with primates and other animals that they will do things for and return favors for one another. Reciprocity, one of the pillars of morality, is not strictly a human attribute.

Although we share the capacity for connectedness with primates, humans also have the capacity to connect to concepts and constructs larger than ourselves, such as organizations and society.

The Evolution of Connectedness

Connectedness is the glue that binds living beings together. Connectedness is what allows us to extend our sensibility and sensitivity, to share experiences with other individuals and social units.

Anthropology has taught us that about 175,000 years ago, in the rift valley of Africa, there were about 10,000 anatomically modern human beings. These were our ancestors. Geneticists have identified a "Database" woman, meaning that her genes have been passed to everyone reading this book and everyone else on the planet. Interestingly, scientists have also identified a "Database" male, referred to as the "Y-Chromosome Adam," whose genes passed to everyone reading this book and everyone else on the planet.

So, we have on our planet more than seven billion people, all struggling with each other and our different views about the world. Yet, we are inextricably, biologically connected. We all came from the same two people. We all share the same biology. We are all related. We are all connected.

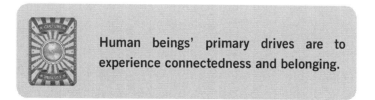

Human beings' primary drives are to experience connectedness and belonging.

Historically, when we lived in forager and hunter communities, communication only extended to the local tribe – basically, how far your voice could carry. Any beings, man or beast, on the other side of the mountain were strangers – different than you. So, connectedness only extended to kin and tribe.

Then, through evolution, humans created the hydraulic and agricultural civilization that changed both our biology and our consciousness. It diminished distances and gave us the experience of more time, bringing more people together to do different specialized tasks (farmers, carpenters, and so on). This created greater perceived behavioral differences between people based on what people did for work and play.

To keep people connected, humans created a construct of theological consciousness. Instead of connection through kin and tribe, society saw association through religious ties. Jews saw Jews as extended family, empathizing with their situations. Christians saw Christians as extended family. Muslims saw Muslims as extended family.

For some today, this theological consciousness continues to create distance between people and serves as an obstacle to connectedness and/or empathy. Although these people are still living on the same planet, sharing very similar (and, often, exactly the same) struggles, their theology creates a perceived difference, separating them from, rather than connecting them to, each other.

During the Industrial Revolution, markets created a construct called the nation state. Britons saw Britons as extended family. Germans saw Germans as extended family. French saw French and Americans saw Americans all as extended family. Before this time, there were no such things as Germany, France, or America. These are constructs. They are constructs that allow us to extend our loyalty, connectedness, and solidarity based on the complex communication and trade revolutions that reduce distance and give us the experience of more time.

So, connectedness has gone from kin and tribe, to religious ties, to national identification. In *The Empathetic Civilization*,[5] Jeremy Rifkin asks an important question: since consciousness has changed over time, can we guide a shift in consciousness to extend our connectedness to (1) the entire human race as an extended family, (2) to other creatures who share in our evolution, and (3) to the planet as our common community? Is it that much of a stretch to imagine that given new technologies (Internet, social media, and so on) we can extend our empathy to all humans who share the same planet? For what reason would we stop at the nation state identity? Wouldn't that be like having stopped at tribal empathy or religious empathy? What do you think would happen if the Earth were attacked by alien invaders determined to take over the planet? Would national boundaries matter? Not in the slightest! All humanity would be bound together through struggle and adversity.

We have already begun to see this extension of empathy beyond national borders with the global generation, also known as the Millennials. Technology has allowed them, in particular, to extend human biology and psychology (connectedness and belonging) to experience viscerally, not just intellectually, the experience of others. This is how the revolutions began in Tunisia, in Egypt, and in Libya. People can share the experience of others all over the world. We have seen the connectedness in global tragedies from earthquakes, to tsunamis, to typhoons. People from unaffected countries send food, water, money, cell phones – anything that might be needed. If humanity were (as Sigmund Freud or Ayn Rand suggested) self-interested, materialistic, and self-serving, there could be no explanation of the global response to any natural disaster or devastating man-made circumstances.

This type of thinking about connectedness will be necessary for organizations, and the people who they employ, to work with them and other organizations. This is the fundamental change that will have to occur for organizations to function collaboratively. The beginning of this shift is already under way in organizations like Google, Zappos, Evernote, and others. Human connectedness is the future direction of business.

Primary and Secondary Human Drives

Since Roman times, there have been theories in political science, in philosophy, and science of *homo homini lupus* or "man is a wolf to man," meaning that deep down inside the nature of human beings, like wolves, lies a nature that is nasty, hostile, aggressive, violent, and competitive. This is very unfair (to the wolf). Wolves by nature are very cooperative animals. It is no accident that we keep their cousins, domesticated dogs, as pets. It's also unfair to humanity, because humans are much more cooperative and connected to one another than many want to believe.

 If we want to build institutions, societies, or cultures that involve connectedness and belonging, we must be willing to discuss the *actual* primary drivers of human behavior.

The true primary drives of humans are to connect and belong. These are referred to as empathetic drives. They are an entirely new frame of reference that challenges our previous assumptions in evolutionary biology, neurocognitive science, and human development. These changes fundamentally change our understanding of human nature and the meaning of human existence. And with these changes, we must also consider the institutions that were built based on prior assumptions, such as educational institutions, financial institutions, business practices, and government.

We know that when we watch a movie, if we are connected to a character in that movie, and we watch that character fall into a pit of snakes, we're going to feel pretty uncomfortable. If the character we are connected to is in a painful or profoundly sad situation, we feel their pain or their sorrow. We may take this type of emotion for granted, but it is evidence that we are actually soft-wired to experience another's condition as our own. Soft wiring refers to a neurological pathway that exists to facilitate action but must be exercised through behavioral rehearsal for it to be intact and effective. This contrasts with hard wiring, which is a neurological pathway that carries a particular action that has become "automatic" through behavioral rehearsal. The emotion we experience through others is because of our mirror neurons.

> **Self-interest, violence, and aggression are secondary drives that arise when our primary drives are stifled in some way.**

Mirror neurons are just the tip of the iceberg of recent findings in neuropsychology and brain research that suggest we are *not* soft-wired for self-interest, aggression, and violence, as previously thought. These are secondary drives. We are soft-wired for attachment, affection, sociability, and companionship. Our primary drive is to connect and belong. We usually only see human secondary drives arise when our primary drives are stifled or short-circuited.

However, as long as we create cultures at the national, regional, and organizational level that see the world as a zero-sum game, we will see the appearance of secondary drives like self-centeredness, materialism, aggression, and violence. As long as we perceive environments to have scarcity rather than abundance, we will override our soft-wiring for our primary drives of human connectedness and belonging.

Understanding what human primary drives are – and what it takes to support them – allows us to build institutions and a society that will maximize connectedness.

Connectedness in Society

To paraphrase certain Eastern philosophies, life is suffering. It's a challenge to live on this planet, whether you are a human navigating the streets of London or an elk navigating the mountains of Colorado. When children become aware of and focus on the vulnerability and fragility of life, they can develop mature empathy for another person or being. Just like they are alive, the other person or being is alive and may be in a difficult circumstance.

When you think about the times that we have felt connected to others, it's because we connect with them through the experience of their struggle, a similar one in our own lives, or one that could potentially affect any one of us. We show unity, as humans, through our connection, belonging, and kindness. We need only to look as far as national or international responses after tragedies such as the events of 9/11, the 2004 Indian Ocean earthquake and tsunami, and the London Underground bombings of 7/7 – and consider the response of so many who were not involved in these events. With each of these events, the majority of the world responded with horror. Many around the world showed unity with the victims, regardless of what country they were from or how far away they lived.

Connectedness is fundamentally the shared experience of the fragility of life, the fact that unforeseen events that we have no control over can happen to any one of us. The sense of connection comes from our ability to share the experiences of those around us, both positive and negative. It's based on the acknowledgment that we are all imperfect and we are all connected through our imperfectness. Each one of us, regardless of our age, gender, ethnicity, race, religion, and socioeconomic status all struggle, in one or more ways, in our lives.

Evidence of how shared struggle connects all of us begins in the first few days of life and continues to evolve as we mature.

The Complexity of Connectedness

Connectedness is a complex phenomenon. If you've ever been in a maternity unit that may have twenty babies in a single room, if one baby starts to cry, what happens? The other babies will also cry. Why? It's referred to as empathic distress. The other babies start to cry because they can experience the distress of the first baby that started to cry. It is built into their biology. We are soft-wired to feel others' experiences.

If you take a child and put that child in front of a mirror, at about 2½ years old (but not before) that child will begin to recognize itself in the mirror. This is when mature empathy begins to develop. This is when the toddler begins to realize *I am a separate being from my mother, my father, and any of these other people who surround me.* It is at about this age that a toddler realizes if something happens to someone else and they feel it, it's because the other person is having the experience.

Depending on nationality and culture, most children begin to learn about birth and death and how each occurs somewhere between the ages of six and eight years old. They learn that they have only one life and that it is fragile and vulnerable, and it is at this age that they learn that eventually, they, like their parents, will die. This is another developmental step.

Studying Connectedness

When children begin to experience the vulnerability and fragility of life, they can truly begin to feel for others. According to Andrew Nicholson, Juanita M. Whalen, and Penny M. Pexman, a group of researchers in the department of psychology at the University of Calgary that published a 2013 study looking at empathy in children,[6] this is also the time that children begin to understand sarcasm (if they are empathetic).

In their study, Nicholson and his colleagues investigated why some children understood sarcasm earlier than others. They suspected that children who were more empathetic (able to connect emotionally to others) might be quicker to recognize the incongruence between what was being said, and the tone and expression of the person saying it.

To test out their hypothesis, the researchers studied 31 children who were between the ages of eight and nine. They asked the children's parents to complete a questionnaire designed to assess each child's level of empathy. Parents were asked, for example, to rate how true the following statements were:

- My child shows concern for someone else who is upset.
- My child likes to rip the legs off of insects.

Not many parents reported that their kids liked to torture insects (which would have been a clear sign that empathy was lacking), and most of them said their children showed concern when someone was upset.

While the parents were filling out their questionnaires, the children were watching snippets from a puppet show, some of which included comments that were sarcastic.

For example, in one scenario involving puppets and snowboarding, one of the puppets is snowboarding in artificial snow. That puppet goes over a jump and lands poorly, falling on his head. The other puppet says, 'That was so *good*.'"

At the end of each snippet, the children were asked to indicate whether the commenting puppet was being mean or nice. To make it easier for the children who might have problems expressing their feelings, Nicholson and his colleagues set up a proxy for each answer – children were to choose a duck toy when they meant "nice" and a shark toy when they meant "mean."

When the researchers correlated the findings with the responses to the puppet shows, they saw a clear role for empathy and connectedness: the more empathetic the children were, the more likely it was that they had correctly identify sarcastic comments in the puppet shows.

Once empathy and connectedness are developed in children, it makes them much more capable of understanding sophisticated expressions, such as sarcasm. Unfortunately, even after developing this level of sophisticated emotional empathy, it doesn't remain constant. When children enter into adolescence, the non-empathetic behaviors we see (such as bullying and indifference to peers based on social group) support the idea that because children may feel essentially immortal at this age, the connection with others diminishes. The feeling of immortality creates distance between adolescents and those who are mere mortals. Adolescents tend to remain emotionally connected to their peer groups because they are "like them," but feel little connection to others outside their peer group. Part of the feeling of connectedness is created by the sense of mortality. During the period of time when young adolescents feel immortal, they are less likely to feel connected to those outside their peer group.

On the other side of adolescence, adults tend to return to the value of connectedness and its benefits. Once we develop this more mature capacity for connectedness, there are a variety of ways to display it.

Channels of Connection

Connectedness can be demonstrated through various channels. Emotional and physical empathy can be shown through synchrony, motor mimicry, or emotional contagion. Taking the perspective of others is a form of empathy that is demonstrated through a cognitive channel.

You have probably noticed that when you speak to someone who is depressed, you will adopt a sad posture and a sad expression, and before you realize it, you will feel sad. This is the body's physical/emotional channel. This is an example of synchrony and motor mimicry, which occurs due to mirror neurons. Dogs can display this as well. Anyone who has owned a dog can tell stories about how when they are upset, their dog also gets upset, or when they are feeling down, their dog also behaves in a subdued manner. This is one reason why so many people have mammals in the home rather than reptiles who don't demonstrate a similar degree of empathy (or, perhaps, any at all).

Synchronization and emotional contagion are considered very primitive forms of connection. They have been in existence for thousands of years.[7] Another simple example is yawn contagion. Through MRIs, scientists have learned that yawn contagion actually activates the same areas in the brain in both people and primates.[8] We know that people who are highly susceptible to yawn contagion are highly empathic and connect easily to others. People who have problems with connecting to others, such as autistic children, do not display yawn contagion. Chimpanzees, watching an animated chimpanzee on a computer screen, display yawn contagion. Yawn contagion is something that we share with other animals and is an example of the body channel of empathy that is universal in mammals.

Taking the perspective of the other person is a cognitive channel. It is what allows us to distinguish between self and other. Few animals can do this, but beyond humans, it has been demonstrated in apes and elephants.[9, 10]

Consolation, the effort to reduce another's emotional distress, can be demonstrated when using the physical channel. A clear example may be when we put our arms around someone after they have experienced a loss. The idea being that, consolation when offered through the body or physical channel has the ability to reduce someone's emotional distress. This is also how empathy is studied in young children. A family member is instructed to act distressed, and researchers observe the response of the child. As with yawn contagion, children who have difficulty with connectedness and yawn contagion, such as autistic children, have difficulty responding to others in distress and offering consolation.[11]

This is also seen in chimps and other animals. For decades it was believed only humans have the capacity to care about the welfare of others. Frans de Waal has shown that this type of caring also extends beyond humans.[12]

Chimps, like humans, do care about the well-being of others, particularly if they are members of the same group. In his "Prosocial by Choice" chimpanzees study,[13] de Waal put two chimpanzees in two cages next to each other. To be rewarded with food, one chimp can choose tokens that can feed himself only or tokens that can feed both chimps. If the chimp chooses the selfish choice (token), only he gets food; if the chimp chooses the prosocial choice (token), they both get food. For the chimp that is choosing the token, it doesn't really matter which token it chooses, because it always gets a reward.

If the other chimp, the partner that is not making a choice, does nothing or just draws attention to themselves, the prosocial choices increase. If the partner becomes hostile or aggressive, as evidenced by using intimidation or spitting water, the prosocial choices go down. The message from one chimp to the other is very clear: If you don't behave well, I won't be prosocial. To ensure that this is intentional behavior, it was demonstrated that if there is no partner, there are far fewer prosocial choices.

Frans de Waal also looked at the concept of fairness in capuchin monkeys.[14] He took two capuchins and put them side-by-side in separate cages, required them to do a task, and rewarded them with cucumbers. The task was to pass a rock from within the cage to the experimenter outside the cage. They each received a cucumber or a grape for completing the same task. When both monkeys completed that task and they were both rewarded with cucumbers, there was no problem. Both monkeys were happy to do the task, even 25 times in a row. However, de Waal also found that if you give the first monkey *grapes* for completing the task and you give the second monkey *cucumbers* for completing the same task, then you create the experience of inequity between them (in the capuchin world, grapes are apparently much yummier and more desirable than cucumbers).

A similar inequity is created if you give the first monkey a cucumber for completing the task, and you give the second monkey a grape for completing the same task. Once the first monkey sees the second monkey get a grape, it will complete the task again (expecting a grape like the one you gave to the second monkey), but if it is given the cucumber, it actually throws the cucumber at the experimenter and shakes the cage in protest. Some people believe that it would only be a real display of fairness if the capuchin receiving the grape would refuse the grape. Sarah Brosnan, a psychology professor at Georgia State University, who has been doing a similar study with chimpanzees, has seen several pairs of chimps where the one receiving the grape will indeed refuse the grape unless the partner also gets a grape. So, monkeys will reject unequal pay.[15] This type of study looking at reciprocity has been done with dogs and birds with same results.

This is the reason that equal pay for equal work is so important: unequal pay violates our human biological sense of reciprocity and fairness. Historically, businesses maintained inequities, for a variety of reasons, through secrecy. As business and society, through the Internet and other media, become more transparent, any business maintaining inequitable pay policies will either have to pay more equitably or risk losing key employees and be unable to recruit new ones.

Although there are many ways to display connectedness, all forms of connectedness rely on a foundation of warmth. In the context of connectedness, warmth means an openness to invite others into a relationship where trust and concern are fundamental.

Connectedness Requires Warmth

In organizations, warmth (the ability to openly display enthusiasm, affection or kindness) leads to trust and connectedness. It is this type of connection that facilitates information sharing, openness, and cooperation. If coworkers can connect with each other – and trust that each will do the right thing, living up to commitments and agreed-upon planning – then execution becomes much easier. This type of connection also allows for the exchange and acceptance of ideas, even if they are different from our own. This type of openness to listening increases the quality and quantity of ideas that are shared within the organization; fear is no longer an obstacle to communication. Critically, connectedness provides the environment and opportunity to change the beliefs of others, not just their behaviors. As a leader, when you connect with others, they follow you because they want to, not because they have to.

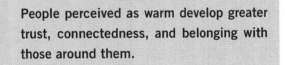

Connectedness is the open display of enthusiasm, affection, or kindness – and it requires warmth. Warmth trumps competence.

In the workplace, most of us are highly invested in demonstrating that we are competent at what we do. Whether our task is to sweep floors, program computers, or lead a team, competence is highly valued. Most of us associate competence with strength, and we want others to see us as we see ourselves: competent and strong. So we do things like work long hours, speak out in meetings, and take on big challenges. Because we are certain of our own desires and intentions, we feel the need to demonstrate competence rather than warmth and connectedness even though warmth fosters connectedness and is more important than competence when it comes to leading others.

People perceived as warm develop greater trust, connectedness, and belonging with those around them.

To build connectedness through warmth, warmth must precede competence. Putting competence first undermines leadership and connectedness. Without using warmth to build connectedness and trust, a leader may have followers complying outwardly with their wishes and requests, but they are much less likely to adopt the values, mission, and culture of the organization in any meaningful way.

 Organizations that lack warmth and connectedness often have a culture of "everyone for themselves."

Andrea Abele of the University of Erlangen-Nuremberg, and Bogdan Wojciszke of the University of Gdansk, are organizational psychologists who have documented people's tendency to focus on competence rather than warmth. In one study, when people were asked to choose between two training programs, one focused on improving competence-related skills (time management, software applications), and the other focused on improving warmth-related skills (social support, listening, communication), most participants chose the competence-related training for themselves and the warmth and the soft-skills training for everybody else. [16]

In another study, when people were asked to tell stories that most defined and influenced the perception of themselves and others, most told stories about themselves that focused on competence ("I received my pilot's license several years ago"), while telling stories about others that focused on warmth and connectedness to others ("My friend is the type of person who will stop if he sees someone on the side of the road to help them change a tire"). [17]

When competence is valued over warmth and trust, an organization's employees are often reluctant to help others because they fear that their efforts will not be reciprocated or recognized – or, even worse, that they will be punished for stepping out of line. People are always anxious and vigilant about protecting their own interests at the expense of everyone else and ultimately the entire organization.

Although most of us continue to overvalue competence over warmth, warmth not only clearly contributes significantly more to how we are evaluated by others, it is also evaluated before competence. Alex Todorov, a social psychologist at Princeton, looked at the cognitive and neural mechanisms that drove our "spontaneous trait inferences," or what we might call "snap judgments" of others.[18, 19] His studies have shown that when people are making judgments of others, particularly regarding with whom they would like to affiliate, they pick warmth before competence. By contrast, when we put competence before warmth, we sacrifice our connectedness to others.

What is it that keeps us from experiencing connectedness to others? What is it that overrides our soft wiring for connectedness, sociability, and collaboration? When we stifle our primary drives (connectedness and belonging), we see our secondary drives (competitiveness, self-centeredness, hostility, and aggression) arise. However, when we see primary drives addressed, our secondary drives are nowhere to be found. In business, when we take money off the table by paying employees fairly and competitively, we create an environment that allows people to focus on things beyond basic survival. It allows our employees to connect with others, collaborate, and work for the collective good of the company and society.

So What?

We have the soft wiring for connectedness. We need to build environments and cultures that bring out our core nature and remove the things that prevent it from being expressed. It is only when our core nature is stifled by ineffective or harmful parenting, education, business practices, culture, and governments that our secondary drives of self-centeredness, materialism, aggression, and violence tend to surface.

This means that, in organizations, if leaders want their employees to offer discretionary effort, they must lead with warmth and connectedness. If leaders want their employees to adopt an "ownership mentality," they must lead with warmth and connectedness. If leaders want their employees to take a global view and make decisions in the best interest of the organization, they must lead with warmth and connectedness.

Connectedness is soft wired into our biology. It now must be hard wired into our institutions and culture.

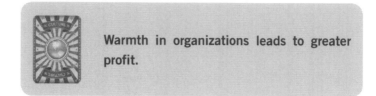

Warmth in organizations leads to greater profit.

It is in our collective interest to begin to think of each other as extended family, connected by history, psychology, and biology, offering unity to each other because we are all tied together by the struggles we all face. To do so, we will have to broaden our identity of inclusion. This does not mean we have to abandon our old identities of nations and religion or blood ties; we just need to extend our connected identities so we can think of all people as sharing the same struggle and experience. Furthermore, particularly since we share part of the same biological and planetary evolution, we can extend the same connection to other creatures as part of our evolutionary family and the planet we all share as our community.

We need to be able to rethink and redefine human nature and realize that if we see behaviors that are outside of our soft-wired biology, outside of our primary drives, it is because of the environments and cultures we have created. We need to build environments and cultures that bring out our connectedness. This will allow us to rethink the cultures that surround us. Like planting a garden, we reap what we sow. We must prepare the culture for business practices and a society based on human connectedness if we want get the most out of the garden we have planted.

Taking Action

1. What is one thing you can do to begin to develop greater connectedness with those around you?

2. At an organizational level, among all of your employees, what can be done to increase connectedness in your culture?

3. Do you prioritize warmth or competence for yourself? Do you prioritize warmth or competence for your employees?

4. What can you do to increase the display of warmth for yourself and among your employees?

CHAPTER 6

TRUST

"The best way to find out if you can trust somebody is to trust them."

– Ernest Hemingway,
Author

What You Need To Know:

1. Trust can be seen in the behaviors of all living things, from microorganisms to humans.

2. Collaboration trumps competition.

3. Trust is a part of the human condition.

4. Trust and anxiety are inversely related.

5. The need for trust is a function of our biology.

6. The world is not a zero-sum game.

7. There is a formula for developing trust.

8. At any particular point in time, an organization can be doing things to develop trust or doing things to undermine it.

9. Trust influences behaviors for both individuals and organizations.

Trust is fundamental to the success of business and personal relationships that are anything more than transactional exchanges. Trust is the belief that the person or entity that you are interacting with will behave in a way that demonstrates reliability, responsiveness, capability, and personal interest. It is necessary if we want our employees to collaborate, innovate, and take appropriate risks.

Many people in business have been taught that business is a zero-sum game, meaning both that rewards are fixed and that one company can only do well at the expense of another. But the real world is not zero-sum, and game theory proves business is not either. Companies such as Zappos, Amazon, Google, and Evernote, just to name a few, prove that in the real world, "a high tide raises all ships." Trust and collaboration can make everyone involved a winner.

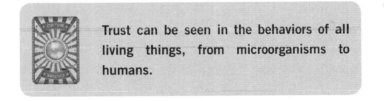

Trust can be seen in the behaviors of all living things, from microorganisms to humans.

We see collaboration all around us in the natural world. We see it in biology and evolution. In a recent study published in November of 2013, in the journal *Astrobiology*,[1] Nora Noffke of Old Dominion University found microbial-induced sedimentary structures (referred to by their acronym, MISS) that show that microbial life existed on earth almost 3.5 billion years ago. These microbes are the oldest life forms that have been identified (so far). The beauty of this finding is that it not only shows the microorganisms, but also the entire ecosystem in which they lived; an ecosystem in which different microbes collaborated and coexisted in order to survive. This means that even in the primordial stew that the earth was 3.5 billion years ago, microbes learned quickly that they would survive better through collaboration in building an ecosystem. As Noffke said, "If cells work together, they have access to a larger set of experiences."

Collaboration trumps competition.

Species that collaborate survive. Sharks don't eat the little fish that have just cleaned their teeth of parasites, when they very easily could. Fig wasps collectively limit the eggs they lay in fig trees; otherwise, the trees would suffer. But why shouldn't any one fig wasp cheat and leave a few more eggs than her rivals? At the level of human society, in many places on the planet, villagers that share a common but finite farming resource do not try to exploit that resource more than others. The path of trust and cooperation is simply more effective for survival and thriving. Sharks, fig wasps, and villagers sharing common areas all cooperate because the relationships they're in are mutually beneficial.

Trust is a factor that can be supported or undermined by organizational culture. In cultures that value and instill trust, you see members willing to take risks, innovate, and collaborate. In cultures where trust is not present, you see members developing adversarial relationships, competing rather than collaborating, and looking out for themselves rather than the organization.

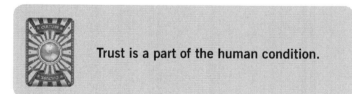 **Trust is a part of the human condition.**

Trust (and distrust) are part of the human condition. Trust affects relationships at every level: individual, family, organizational, national, and international. The experience of trust (or distrust) is directly associated with a human emotional experience, which is biologically hardwired into our brains: the experience of anxiety. Anxiety and trust are inversely related. Whether on a global, national, or organizational stage, anxiety undermines trust. Conversely, trust can reduce anxiety. This means the less trust we have in a person, leader, organization or country, the more anxiety we will feel. Conversely, the more trust we have in a person, leader, organization, or country, the less anxiety we experience in that relationship.

Trust vs. Anxiety

Anxiety has long been studied in the fields of evolutionary biology and psychology. It exists because of the biological function of our brain. These areas of study have taught us that anxiety, while felt throughout our body, occurs in our brain. It also exists in other animals as a result of the evolutionary development in their brains.

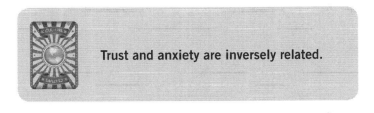

Trust and anxiety are inversely related.

Within the human brain, there are three parts:

1. *The reptilian brain.* Evolutionarily the oldest part of our brain, the reptilian brain dates back as far 200 million years. It's similar to the brain possessed by the reptiles that preceded mammals. It's "preverbal" but controls life functions such as the autonomic brain, which includes breathing, heart rate, and the fight/flight/freeze response. Lacking language, its impulses are instinctual and ritualistic. It's concerned with fundamental needs such as survival, physical maintenance, hoarding, dominance, territory, preening, and mating. This brain structure is also found in less evolutionarily complex life forms such as lizards, crocodiles, and birds.

2. *The limbic brain.* This part of the brain first evolved in mammals. It remembers pleasant and unpleasant behaviors. It is responsible for our experience of emotions. It includes a brain structure called the amygdala, which is particularly responsible for our experience of fear.

3. *The neocortex.* This part of the brain was first seen in primates and plays a dominant role in the human brain. It is what makes us human. It is responsible for language, abstract thought, imagination, and creativity. This is where culture, both human and organizational, resides.

Anxiety is the physiological state that prepares both humans and animals to respond to threat. It can be seen physiologically in increased heart rate, increased blood pressure, vascular dilation, increased muscle tension, and a shot of cortisol in the blood stream (all to prepare for action), as well as increased pupil dilation (to increase perception). These physiological responses are what feed into the reptilian part of the brain and ultimately translate into a fight, flight, or freeze response.

When a person or animal perceives a threat, it's the amygdala that signals the reptilian part of the brain to prepare the body for fight, flight, or freeze. It is the neocortex, the highest and most sophisticated part of our brain, that interprets the nuance of the threat and can regulate the response of the amygdala. If you know people who are "perched and ready to leap" (people who are typically very angry or always seem like they are ready to respond in a hostile way), I like to think of them as living in their reptilian brain, not effectively using their higher-functioning neocortex.

The experience of anxiety (and its closely related emotional brethren, including fear, nervousness, worry, concern, apprehension, tension, angst, and impending doom), has existed in humans and other animals for hundreds of thousands of years. Anxiety is rooted in our biology, specifically in the amygdala, which lies in the limbic system.

The amygdala is a part of the brain responsible for vigilance. It is constantly on, all the time, trying to spot potential threats. These responses were evolutionarily very adaptive (or they wouldn't still be with us). They occur quickly, without requiring a lot of high-level, precise assessment of a situation. The amygdala responds to a threat threshold. If a threat level is crossed, anxiety is created and sends a signal to the reptilian part of our brain creating a fight (the possibility of a physical confrontation to defend itself), flight (to run away from the threat), or freeze (to become frozen or immobile in the hopes that the threat may pass by without the person or animal being detected as a possible meal) reaction. This functioned well historically because when early humans roamed the planet, we may have been early hunters, but we were also prey. If we stumbled upon a saber tooth tiger, we didn't have the luxury of thinking, "Hmmm ... can I eat it or can it eat me?" We just needed to react to the threat. Humans that survived those chance encounters did so because of their amygdala and anxiety response, and passed those down to each of us.

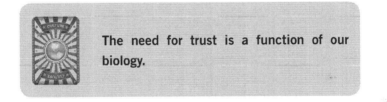

The need for trust is a function of our biology.

In the 21st century, our modern challenge is that the biological hardwiring — the anxiety response — that we had 100,000 years ago is still with us today, whether the threat is real or perceived. But most of the threats we face on a day-to-day basis are not black or white or life-threatening. Most threats today are much more nuanced, even when our biology responds as if they were not.

A person might call a friend or their boss and not get a return phone call immediately. They may not think anything of it after two hours. After four hours they may begin to worry. After eight hours, their amygdala might perceive the situation as a real threat, working them into the anxiety associated with full-crisis mode.

Culture can keep people in this high arousal state, through threats of potential termination or public humiliation and the like. It can also reduce this level of threat through transparency, openness, and communication. Even people who have a hostile disposition can learn to function effectively in a culture where threat and hostility are not acceptable.

Perception and Stress

As Shakespeare's Hamlet once observed, "there is nothing good or bad, but thinking makes it so." This means that the world cannot affect us without us drawing some interpretation or conclusion about the world first. Danger is real; threat is perceived. This means that the perception of threat and its corresponding anxiety and stress is something we create. This is what allows two different people to be in the exact same (or very similar) situations and respond completely differently.

For example, if you and I are standing at the top of a snow-covered mountain, looking down the same slope, you may think, *I can't ski this. This run is way over my head. I'm going to die.* I may think, *Conditions are great today, and anything is skiable in these conditions. This is going to be an awesome run.* Same situation, different thoughts (assessments) about the situation, different conclusions and emotional responses to the situation. In this example, you would feel a much higher level of anxiety and stress, triggering a fight, flight, or freeze response, while I would feel a much lower level of stress, likely allowing me to relax and enjoy the situation much more.

We know that all this happens because anxiety and stress are a response to our thinking and assessment in the moment. It requires two lines of thinking: (1) the overestimation of threat *and* (2) the underestimation of our ability to deal with that threat. A negative assessment of both these perspectives creates anxiety and stress.

These high-stress responses to real or perceived threat situations create a real problem. Dr. Herbert Benson of the Benson-Henry Institute for Mind Body Medicine at Massachusetts General Hospital and Beth Israel Deaconess Medical Center published an article in May of 2013, in the journal *PLOS ONE*.[2] In part, he and his team supported the existing research literature, finding that the stress response in human beings can lead to psychological disorders such as anxiety and depression, as well as physical conditions such as hypertension, cardiovascular disease, various inflammatory diseases, and certain cancers that are exacerbated by stress.

What is new from his study is that people who were able to create a relaxation response for themselves (using techniques such as mantra meditation, yoga poses, or prayer) could now distance themselves from the thoughts that had previously created a threat and a stress response. This new mental environment not only arrested, but actually reversed, the adverse effects of the stress response. Specifically, Dr. Benson said that people who were able to use these techniques to create a relaxation response through creating this specific mental environment had "a specific genomic response that counteracts the harmful genomic effects of stress."

People who could create this relaxation response activated genes that improved energy metabolism, mitochondrial function, insulin secretion, telomere maintenance, and reduced expression of genes linked to inflammatory response and other stress-related responses. This is the first time that any study has been able to prove that these various ways of achieving a relaxation response have observable, measurable, biological effects.

To be clear, the study indicated explicitly that these effects are *not* because these practices are changing genes. They are changing the *expression* of the genes (epigenetics). Interestingly, they saw positive effects with subjects who were taught these techniques as early as eight weeks after they initiated practice. Also, those that had been practicing routinely for years had greater positive results, suggesting the effects are not only long-term but also cumulative.

When we learn to create an environment that allows us to trigger a relaxation response in the face of an otherwise potentially threatening, stressful situation, not only do we experience less anxiety and stress, but the results are positive for us psychologically and biologically.

I'm not suggesting we need to change the situations that create stress; we don't always have the possibility of doing so in the moment. We need to learn a new habit pattern of thinking and of adjusting our perception of the situation. When we are members of a culture where we can trust ourselves and those around us, we have a decreased experience of anxiety and stress. When the culture in which we live and work supports trust, it reduces the perception of threat, and facilitates risk-taking and collaboration.

To leverage collaboration in an organization, we must understand the conditions that facilitate it and those that serve as an obstacle to it. We also need to understand the specific strategies that maximize collaboration. These are both demonstrated in the classic game called The Prisoner's Dilemma.

Collaboration: The Prisoner's Dilemma

In 1950, Merrill Flood and Melvin Dresher invented a classic game called The Prisoner's Dilemma.[3] This game was later used by Dr. Robert Axelrod to understand the nature of trust, cooperation, and their effects on competition.[4]

Here's how it works. Two participants in the game/experiment are "captured" and "taken prisoner" by a hostile group and then separated by their "captors." Prisoner A and Prisoner B are then made an offer (separately) by their captors: betray the other person (perhaps by sharing information), and receive a lighter punishment. Unable to communicate with one another, each of them is now tempted to betray the other in exchange for more favorable treatment.

In the game, players are explained the above scenario and points are assigned based on the responses of each prisoner. If both Prisoner A and Prisoner B remain loyal, both refusing to betray the other, they each receive three "points" (points in this case are used only symbolically, to indicate advantage). If one betrays (defects) and the other does not, the one who betrays receives five points, and the one who did not receives zero points. If both betray each other (defect), both receive one point.

The game is played for several rounds, and at the end, the points are tallied to see who and what strategies create the greatest points (gains).

Consider this scenario from the point of view of Prisoner A:

- "If I remain loyal to Prisoner B, my best-case-scenario is three, and my worst-case scenario is zero."
- "If I betray Prisoner B, my best case-scenario is five, and worst is one."
- "Therefore, either way, I am better off betraying Prisoner B. Defecting is always better than cooperating."

Meanwhile, Prisoner B is coming to the same conclusion: that it is always better to defect. Through this thought process, both parties are encouraged to defect.

In a world where interactions are singular or transactional, this strategy may make perfect sense. What is the reason to collaborate if defecting provides a better outcome in the short term? However, in business and in life, as well as in the Prisoner's Dilemma, relationships are not transactional. You are playing for several rounds. As a result, the interaction is not transactional (single occurrence) but relational (requiring repeated interactions, allowing for accumulated experience).

In trying to find a solution to what behavioral strategy would be best in this type of situation, several questions may arise:

- What are some of the strategies for interacting in this competitive context?
- When should we cooperate?
- When should we defect?
- Is there a balance between cooperating too much (being a "sucker") and defecting too much (being a "bully")?

The Winning Strategy

To explore these questions, Dr. Axelrod asked mathematicians, behavioral theorists, and political scientists to offer strategies for the best way to play this game. They developed many complex strategies that took into account different variables, one being learning styles.

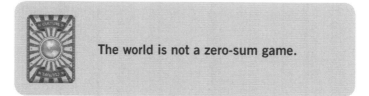

The world is not a zero-sum game.

However, it turned out that the single most effective strategy was also the simplest, and it was developed by a computer: "tit-for-tat." The strategy consists of just two simple maneuvers:

1. Cooperate on the first move (you risk first!).
2. On following moves, do whatever the other player did.

The strategy is distinguished by the following characteristics:

1. *It is vulnerable.* Those who employ the tit-for-tat strategy are never the first to defect. Vulnerability is critical to building a trustful environment, developing a reliable reputation, and facilitating success.
2. *It is responsive.* When the other party defects (exploits), the first party responds immediately and clearly.
3. *It is forgiving.* If the other party backs off, then the first party responds in kind ("let bygones be bygones").
4. *It is fair.* One party does not try to gain advantage over the other party.
5. *It is simple.* This is not a complex theory or chess game. The tit-for-tat strategy requires little strategic planning. It is cooperative without applying any trickery.

These are characteristics that are necessary in a culture with trust. Vulnerability requires us to take risks. Responsiveness requires us to be aware of and attentive to how other parties respond to our behavior. Forgiveness allows us to focus on the future when something goes wrong, without getting stuck on past missteps. Simplicity ensures that everyone in our culture can understand and behave consistently.

Some of the surprising principles that have been discovered to govern the "tit for tat" strategy are:

1. *Trust and cooperation can develop even between parties who are self-centered and motivated by self-interest.* Reciprocity is a powerful influencer of behavior even among self-centered people and people who are concerned with self-preservation. Nonetheless, there are two important conditions that must exist for this strategy to work.

    a. Individuals must be able to understand that the re sponse comes from the other person in the interaction and have memory of the outcome.

    b. Both parties must see the interaction as relational, rather than just transactional. If both parties believe they are "in this together," they both have an incentive to build a trusting and cooperative relationship. If the relationship is near its end – or is merely transactional – one might be more apt to defect. Trust comes from the light of the future that casts a shadow on the present.

2. *Cooperation does not require foresight or communication.* It just requires both parties to be able to experience the results of the tit-for-tat strategy. In essence, your response becomes your communication.

3. *Tit-for-tat is a robust strategy.* Within a culture, the strategy of reciprocity spreads quickly. As one party continually models it (beginning with a cooperative move), the other party can quickly discern the pattern. They adopt the strategy themselves.

If there are a lot of members involved in the culture, it doesn't take long for reciprocity to spread to everyone. All that is required is that a few people model it at the outset.

4. *A person applying a reciprocity strategy can never score better than the other person.* This means the competitive concept of winning must be abandoned. Reciprocity and collaboration work for everyone involved without favoring some at the cost of others. From a short-term perspective, use of this strategy does not win any rounds. But from a long-term perspective, it allows all parties come out ahead.

As long as countries, organizations, and people believe that life is a zero-sum game, where someone must "win" and someone must "lose," tit-for-tat strategies, while proven to be effective in generating mutually desirable outcomes, will not be sustainable. When countries, organizations, and people see the world as providing abundance rather than scarcity, we can begin to recognize that we don't just have to share this one small piece of pie; together, we can make the pie bigger. This is the cultural shift that will need to take place for collaborative strategies to take root.

The question then becomes, what are the behaviors we must focus on to create this cultural shift? If our goal is to increase trust in order to, in turn, reduce anxiety and increase collaboration, it is critical that we identify the most powerful levers at our disposal.

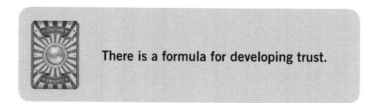

There is a formula for developing trust.

When looking at the level of trust in an organization, I suggest you consider the following formula:

$$\text{Trust} = \frac{\text{Experience}}{\text{Risk}}$$

When you consider the formula above, it indicates that in order to increase trust, the two variables you must consider are experience and risk. Because experience is in the numerator, and risk is in the denominator, if you want to increase trust, experience must grow faster and more significantly than risk.

Imagine the following two scenarios:

- *Scenario 1:* You are in one of my full-day workshops. It's time to break for lunch, for which we all have one hour. You come up to ask me a question. After I answer your question, I casually say to you, "I left my wallet in my hotel room. Is there any way I can borrow $5 for lunch? I'll make sure I get it back to you." You have known me (experience) for about four hours. For most people, parting with $5 with the possibility of not getting it back does not represent a huge loss (risk). So, most people would say, "Yes" – and offer the $5.

- *Scenario 2:* You are in one of my full-day workshops. It's time to break for lunch, for which we all have one hour. You come up to ask me a question. After I answer your question, I casually say to you, "I'm about to buy a house and I'm a little short on the down payment. Could I borrow $50,000? I'll make sure I get it back to you." Here again, you have known me (experience) for about four hours. However, for most people, parting with $50,000 with the possibility of not getting it back (risk) is much greater. So, they are likely to say, "Sorry. I can't help you." If you want people to trust you, when you ask them to take risks for you, personally or professionally, you must ensure they have enough experience with you to overcome the sense of risk they feel, and it must be experience of a specific kind.

If you were going to build a house, you would first want to ensure it had a solid foundation. To ensure your house had that solid foundation, would you build that foundation on sand or rock? Most people would prefer rock. Rock is solid, immovable, and lasting.

In the organizational model I suggest, trust is also built on a foundation of rock, or ROCC. Each letter represents one of the behaviors that create the experience necessary to overcome risk and build trust.

So the new equation looks like:

$$\text{Trust} = \frac{\text{Experience (ROCC)}}{\text{Risk}}$$

According to the Mishra Model for Organizational Trust, trust is developed by four specific behaviors: Reliability, Openness, Competence, and Concern.[5] These are defined as follows:

- *Reliability* is determined by whether or not a person, co-worker, team, supplier, or organization acts consistently and dependably. Do their actions match their words? Can they be counted on to behave in a way that is consistent and reliable with what they have said?
- *Openness* is most often used when people are asked what contributes to organizational trust. This is a dimension of trust that not only involves the accuracy of information that is shared, but also the direct and guileless way in which it is communicated.
- *Competence* is the extent to which we see the people that surround us, such as our friends, co-workers and leaders, as having the ability to effectively accomplish the tasks before them. On

an organizational level, it is a measure of our belief that our organization will be able to compete and thrive.

- *Concern* for employees includes the feelings of connectedness, caring, and benevolence. The idea that organizational leaders care about the conditions of their employees, rather than see them as interchangeable components of a machine, contributes to high trust levels and the discretionary effort all employers seek from their employees.

In organizations where leadership is focused on cash and the bottom line, leaders expect reliability and competence from their employees ... and sometimes offer it in return. In organizations that focus on culture, understanding that profits are an outcome measure of good performance within a good culture, you see all four factors (reliability, openness, competence, and concern) being offered in *both* directions, from employer to employee and vice versa.

> At any particular point in time, an organization can be doing things to develop trust or doing things to undermine it.

Trust is not a static construct. At any particular point in time, an organization can be doing things to develop trust or doing things to undermine it. An excellent example is Hewlett-Packard (HP), which serves both as a model for the creation of trust – and as a cautionary tale regarding how to destroy it. HP is a company that has a long and storied history. From this history, much can be learned regarding how trust affects organizations.

HP is a powerful illustration of how much a culture can influence the success of an organization, large or small. Although HP began as a small company, it was its culture that propelled it to grow, innovate, and become a player on the world stage. It was also a change in culture that led to the challenges it faces today.

In this example, HP's performance closely follows its changes in culture, from an engineering culture to a culture focused on its CEO and on short-term, bottom-line profit, at the expense of investments in its future. More importantly, it demonstrates that when a CEO or business leader forsakes culture for quarterly profits, that CEO or leader makes short-term decisions that jeopardize the company's long-term success, culture, and well-being.

A Star Is Born: The Establishment of the "HP Way"

In 1938, two friends, graduates of Stanford University, decided to work together to start a company. They rented a flat at 367 Addison Avenue, in Palo Alto, near where they had gone to school. The flat was simple and unassuming, and it had a one-car garage, 18x12 ft., with a poured concrete floor and a workbench. That was it. The home at this address, and in particular the garage, would ultimately become a national landmark.

In that garage in 1939, Bill Hewlett and Dave Packard started the company that today is internationally known as Hewlett-Packard (HP). Their first product was an audio oscillator, an electronic test instrument used by sound engineers. One of HP's first customers was Walt Disney Studios, which purchased eight oscillators to develop and test an innovative sound system for the movie *Fantasia*.

They started in a garage with $538 and created a global company. Their genius did not come from the tools they had or didn't have; it came from creating a culture for themselves and those around them where drive, commitment, and desire to create something important were all valued. The garage became a symbol of ingenuity and creativity. Their innovation was building a culture that required a willingness to take a risk – and sometimes even fail.

This culture and management style would become known as the "HP Way." In Bill Hewlett's words, the HP Way is "a core ideology ...

which includes a deep trust and respect for the individual, a dedication to affordable quality and reliability, a commitment to community responsibility, and a view that the company exists to make technical contributions for the advancement and welfare of humanity."

The following tenets were codified as the "HP Way":

1. Trust and respect individuals.
2. Achieve a high level of a contribution.
3. Conduct business with uncompromising integrity.
4. Achieve our common objectives through teamwork.
5. Encourage flexibility and innovation.
6. Create and maintain flat management hierarchy.

These are some of the proven tenets for a culture of success. They are the cultural principles that calm our biologically-wired anxieties when they get triggered by variability in the ever-changing business environment. This culture set Hewlett-Packard apart from its competitors for many years.

Throughout its history, Hewlett-Packard had created and sustained a culture that continued to value trust, respect, and an environment run by engineers focused on creativity and the overall performance of the company. It had done so by mastering the difficult balance of spending enough on research and development to come up with new products, while also making lots of money on the old ones. From its inception, HP modeled these principles – which many other Silicon Valley companies strove to imitate. It had developed a reputation of simply being a company founded by good men, drawing in good employees, and building good products – but it was the culture that created the results. The culture would allow for nothing less than attracting great people and great performance. Unfortunately, when the culture shifted, so did the people and the performance.

By the mid-1990s, the "HP Way" was known worldwide as a model for entrepreneurial corporate culture. It is because of these guiding principles that today HP is identified as the "godfather of Silicon

Valley." Over time, the "HP Way" became synonymous with a culture that embraced flexible work hours, creative freedom, great employee benefits, and a sense that layoffs would be used as only a "last resort." In exchange for this positive culture, employees gave their all to the company, even taking pay cuts to avoid layoffs and remaining loyal when other job offers came their way.

A Half-Century of Success: Reaping the Rewards of the "HP Way"

Under the leadership of CEO Lewis E. Platt, who joined the company in 1992 and was committed to sustaining the "HP Way," HP became the fastest-growing PC maker in the world. The company grabbed third place in the PC market-share war, behind only Compaq and IBM.

In the mid-1990s, HP had five major divisions: computer systems, customer support, IT services, Internet solutions, and printers/personal information products. Like many IT companies at the time, HP experienced the same competitive tensions as other companies and did what it could do to reduce costs across all of its business units. HP was not immune to moving jobs overseas. This was true in the area of manufacturing, customer support, finance, and human resources. HP also found itself reducing employee services, such as employee IT services and human resources support.

While it stands to reason that these economic decisions may have strained employee trust within an organization that had previously been so generous with its employees, an analysis by Elsbach, Stigliani, and Stroud suggests that it was not the cost-cutting measures that led to a loss of employee trust; it was the cultural shift in values that accompanied the cost cutting and what was communicated with that shift that was central to the loss of trust among HP employees.

From 1995 to 1998, under the leadership of Lewis E. Platt, HP was hailed in a variety of publications for making decisions that continued to demonstrate the value and culture of the "HP Way," demonstrating a strong trust and respect for the employees working at HP. For example, at a time when HP received a Distinguished Partner in Progress Award for its operations in Singapore, several employees were interviewed and discussed the trust and respect that HP and its leaders showed for its employees. Most importantly to these employees, the company and its leaders gave them the independence and autonomy to decide how their work was going to get done. To them, this was an expression of respect for employees' integrity and trust in their ability to meet established goals.

It was this type of respect that served as the reason why 47 of the original 62 employees at HP Singapore had remained at HP since starting their jobs 25 years prior.

There were other HP programs that drew media attention at that time. Hewlett-Packard Ireland designed a program that offered employees flexibility in their work schedules and this program was also a focus of attention. For the employees, these programs served as evidence that they lived and worked in a culture that trusted employees' ability to use their time effectively.

Moreover, HP demonstrated a culture with strong camaraderie. Many employees referred to the company being "a close-knit family" and "a second home."

Between 1995-1998, prior to HP's #10 ranking in the *Fortune* magazine "100 Best Companies to Work For" survey, the popular media effusively detailed the cultural norms within HP and how HP leaders put into practice the "HP Way." This was illustrated through leadership decisions that demonstrated trust and respect for employees. They were viewed as building integrity between what leadership said and what it did. The expression of these cultural norms came not only from the leaders but also from the employees who happily discussed these programs and policies.

This period of time was the cultural Mount Everest for HP. It should surprise no one that during this time, employee trust was extremely high. This was reflected in the high ranking in the *Fortune* survey and in HP's stock performance, which hit its peak of $76.50 shortly after

Platt's departure from HP. Unfortunately, all of this was all about to change.

The Beginning of the End: New CEO
Signals the End of the "HP Way"

On July 19, 1999, shortly before the retirement of Lewis Platt, the CEO who had headed HP for seven years, HP announced that it had found and selected its next CEO. HP had selected an outsider, Carly Fiorina, the former director of Lucent Technology's Global Services business unit, to be its new CEO. This stunned many industry analysts. HP had only rarely selected management from outside its culture, particularly when considering its top management positions. The new CEO had a well-established reputation for being highly competitive (rather than collaborative), which put her style of leadership in direct conflict with HP's culture, the "HP Way."

It was not long before Fiorina took her first missteps. She began to send clear signals that there would be cultural changes coming, and she could not wait to make those changes. Shortly after her appointment, Fiorina made several decisions and statements that were seen as demonstrating contempt for HP's culture and its employees.

For example, in a National Public Radio interview on July 19, 1999, shortly after her appointment, Fiorina said, "I think in general, the people of HP would agree that we need to increase our sense of urgency, reinvigorate our competitive spirit, and focus on speed."[6] In addition, while speaking at the high-tech Comdex conference later that fall, Fiorina talked about "reinventing" HP by taking more risks and moving faster.

These statements, taken together, displayed a real lack of appreciation for the "HP Way," the culture that had made HP so successful to that point. Fiorina's statements communicated to the successful employees of HP that there was something clearly wrong with the culture at HP – and she was there to fix it. This was tantamount to saying to the goose that laid the golden eggs, "Your eggs aren't gold enough. They should be larger and be produced more quickly."

This was the beginning of the end of the "HP Way." Industry experts and observers agreed that the long-standing traditions of employee trust, respect, and collaboration among engineers and other creative types would see a rapid decline under Fiorina. Sadly, they were right.

On January 10, 2000, HP fell from #10 to #43 on *Fortune's* annual survey of the "100 Best Companies to Work For."[7] Clearly informed about the discomfort and nervousness among HP employees regarding the company's next steps, *Fortune* wrote: "New CEO Carly Fiorina promised that the new, streamlined HP she would 'Invent' would remain true to the culture of integrity and respect known as the 'HP Way.' Even as Fiorina promised to maintain 'integrity and respect' for the 'HP Way,' her actions continued to suggest that the old 'HP Way' would not last and that current ways of doing business at HP were unacceptable."

The theme "Invent" became the center of Fiorina's new global advertising campaign in the summer of 2000, with Fiorina serving as narrator. This initiated the "CEO as Rock Star" culture. Fiorina became the face of the company, rather than its engineers and its business units. The campaign was about her, not the company.

Fiorina's overarching goal was to centralize authority over all HP business units.[8] This undermined the culture of autonomy, which allowed leaders of each business unit to do what was best for the company and their own unit. Fiorina's campaign also undermined the "HP Way." The clear message was that prior ad campaigns, allowing individual focus on business units, were inadequate, thereby ignoring and diminishing previous successes. At a minimum, this uniform ad campaign, with Fiorina as its face, undervalued HP's existing brand strength, and at most, it ignored it completely.

If there were any questions about this, they were answered when she placed her own portrait next to the portraits of Bill Hewlett and Dave Packard.[9] HP had had other CEOs, and none had placed their portraits alongside those of the founders. HP employees considered this tantamount to sacrilege.

The most troubling part is that, at the time, HP was performing well. The need to remake and "Invent" the HP culture was not evident to employees. However, on January 8, 2001, *Fortune* published its next "100 Best Companies to Work For" list. HP was #63.[10] The *Fortune* ranking was a symptom of the widespread dissatisfaction with the leadership and how any cultural shift was being imposed.

Compaq Merger: The Final Nail in the Coffin of the "HP Way"

Unbeknownst to HP employees at the time, Fiorina's master plan involved making HP an alternative to IBM for big business. She planned to do this through a merger with Compaq. This would require her to use the "HP Way" against employees in a series of deceptive moves, and the true motivation underlying these moves would only become clear after the fact.

On April 19, 2001, HP reported that their earnings were severely down and pay bonuses and raises would be suspended, while managerial staff would be cut. In July 2001, employees were asked to take voluntary pay cuts to avert layoffs. This would only be fathomable if management could rely on what remained of the original "HP Way," "Trust," and "People first – We're all in this together." In August 2001, HP laid off 6,000 employees anyway, after all had taken a pay cut.[11]

The reduction of salaries and HP staff allowed Fiorina to reduce the documented liabilities on HP's balance sheet before the Compaq merger. This would put HP in a more favorable position during negotiations prior to the merger. To Fiorina, this may have seemed like a perfectly reasonable business decision.

To HP employees, who were at the time unaware of her intention to merge HP with Compaq, this was a betrayal. This severely undercut Fiorina's integrity and credibility. Understandably, employees felt burned and taken advantage of. The culture no longer had a "people first" priority, and leadership could not be trusted to follow through on its commitments to employees.

On September 4, 2001, HP announced it had plans to merge with the world's largest PC maker, Compaq Computer Corporation, based in Houston, Texas. From the onset of the announcement, reports indicated that the merger would result in at least 15,000 lost jobs and "a new culture at HP that would focus on sales and services, rather than engineering innovation."[12]

This was precisely the cultural shift imposed by Fiorina and the Board that continues to plague HP to this day. Trust in the engineers that built the company and made it successful, and in their employees' ability to innovate, collaborate, and create, would all be replaced by a sales-driven organization.

On September 6, 2001, the *New York Times* revealed that Fiorina and the Board's real goal was to become an "alternative to IBM."[13] This would create not only a change in culture, but a change in identity. HP would move from being producer of specialized computing products to being a large corporate force in information technology.

This shift was protested widely by observers, analysts, and especially HP employees. Everyone who was familiar with HP saw this as the final death knell of the "HP Way," and also a lack of appreciation for the creativity of the HP engineering culture.

As a consequence of this change in direction, Fiorina began to raid the research and development budget to try to keep HP's quarterly numbers looking good for Wall Street. Research and development had always created the future for HP. When you stop investing in the future to bolster your appearance in the present, you sacrifice both the present and the future. Again, this was shortsighted and continues to plague HP to this day.

On November 11, 2001, David Packard, board member and eldest son of one of the founders of Hewlett-Packard, sent a letter to HP shareholders opposing the merger. This initiated a well-publicized proxy fight. Packard was opposing the merger based on the predicted loss of 15,000 jobs, which he said would be outside the founders' values. Packard's letters indicated that HP's leadership did not value its employees.

In response to Packard's letter, HP began a series of attacks on Mr. Packard using news releases as the means of communication. These news releases had the consistent message that HP needed to change if it was going to remain competitive. The news releases alternated between two points: (1) those opposing the merger were described as "retreating into the past," "using an incremental approach," and "attempting in vain to preserve the status quo"; and (2) those supporting the merger were described as "taking bold steps," "withstanding challenges," and "charging ahead." Both these messages communicated the same thing to employees who had been with HP for years and made it successful. It communicated to them clearly: *the culture you have is not worth saving.* This created a greater chasm of trust between the leaders and employees of HP.

On February 4, 2002, *Fortune* published its next "100 Best Companies to Work For" list. HP was completely off the list.[14] In addition, in the shareholder showdown, the meeting where the merger would be voted on, Walter Hewlett, son of co-founder Bill Hewlett (and, like David Packard, opposed to the merger), received a standing ovation, while Carly Fiorina received boos.

Nonetheless, the merger was approved by a small margin, and both the merger and the layoffs would occur. Fiorina moved forward with her new company, knowing full well that many of the employees she was leading voted against the direction she had chosen.

The lack of trust and apparent lack of integrity were expressed in various publications describing the disappointment from industry experts and employees alike. All lamented the loss of the "HP Way" that would be replaced by the "New HP." Historically, HP leaders had always worked with employees to move the company in a direction that was mutually beneficial. That was part of the trust and collaboration mandate in the culture. The HP-Compaq merger displayed to the whole world that this was an entirely different company with an entirely different leadership. This action was proof that employees simply mattered less to leadership than they had in the past. This was the fundamental shift.

Fiorina Forced Out: The Reign of Terror Finally Comes to an End

In 2002, after the merger, while Fiorina found herself leading a divided company, she was often quoted as saying, "The wisdom of this decision will become more and more evident over time."[15] These words would be her undoing.

In 2003, HP did not return to *Fortune's* "100 Best Companies to Work For" list. The same was true in 2004. For the third quarter of 2004, it became clear that profits would be well below Wall Street expectations. In response to the poor performance, Fiorina, calling performance "unacceptable," fired three executives responsible for the computer server and storage unit.

Now that analysts had two years of data to look at post-merger, it became clear that although the merger did indeed cut costs, it produced none of the synergies that were promised by Fiorina in 2002.

On February 9, 2005, while some were calling for the break-up of the merger, Carly Fiorina, CEO for the past five years, was forced to step down. The board named Robert Wayman, chief financial officer and a 36-year Hewlett-Packard employee, as interim CEO.

Since Carly Fiorina was fired, HP has had three other CEOs: Mark Hurd, 2005-2010, Leo Apotheker, 2010-2011, and Meg Whitman, 2011-present. Each one has had difficulty reestablishing trust with HP employees. As discussed in an earlier chapter, once social norms (trust being one part) are lost, they are exceedingly difficult to reestablish.

Lessons Learned

The future of HP remains in question even today. It is clear that although HP once offered a model of organizational culture that many followed, culture is a dynamic force that can and does change based on competitive market conditions and leadership.

Trust influences behaviors for both individuals and organizations.

For half a century, HP offered a culture based on trust, collaboration, engineering innovation, and a high value for its people. It was this culture that sustained it as an organization and continued to create its future. It was only when a new CEO radically changed its culture that HP began to decline.

It took several years for HP to feel the full effects of its change in direction. Unfortunately, it continues to suffer the ill effects of that shift even today. Once trust in the leaders of an organization is lost, it is difficult to recapture.

A culture imbued with trust is difficult to create, but the evidence of its positive results lie in the first 50 years of HP success. The formula for trust discussed earlier in this chapter gives any organization the tools to establish a culture of trust between leaders and employees. This is a major component of culture that will create benefits and profits for the organization, its leaders, and its employees.

So What?

In the context of defining and developing trust, if you now look back at the actions taken by Carly Fiorina as CEO of HP, you can see how she was a wonderful example of all the things you should *not* do when initiating a culture change. You can also see how all the behaviors that would support trust were violated.

Consider the equation from earlier in this chapter:

$$\text{Trust} = \frac{\text{Experience (ROCC)}}{\text{Risk}}$$

Let's look, specifically, at where Fiorina went wrong:

1. *Reliability.* Fiorina's reliability and integrity were called into question when she made statements indicating that HP employ-

ees were important to her, while taking actions that indicated they were not. Nowhere was this more evident than in July of 2001, when employees were asked to accept reduced wages in order to avert layoffs. They did. In August of 2001, 6,000 employees were laid off anyway.

Reliability is one of the most fundamental behaviors in establishing trust. Most leaders look for reliability in their employees' performance. Employees look for reliability in their leaders' words. Your words and behaviors must have congruence. If there is incongruence between the two, you will be perceived as unreliable and untrustworthy, your employees will experience greater anxiety and stress, and performance will decrease because employees will be more worried about watching their own backs than anything else they are supposed to be doing.

2. *Openness.* Fiorina's openness was called into question when one month after laying off 6,000 employees (and promising layoffs could be averted by taking pay cuts the month before that) she announced a merger with Compaq and a change in direction for HP. This had been her goal from the beginning, and it was not information that was shared with any engineers in the company.

   In today's society, openness is referred to as transparency. In large organizations in particular, there is often a perception that "information is power." In other words, those with information are powerful; those without it are not. The problem with this type of culture is that information is typically withheld from those that most need it. In a transparent and open culture, information is shared freely and collaboration thrives because of it.

   Information in an organization is like air. It should be shared as openly as possible. The more that it is shared, the more the company grows.

3. *Competence.* Fiorina's competence was suspect when she shifted a previously successful HP from an engineering company to

a sales-focused company, stripping money from research and development and initiating a merger with Compaq.

Competence is a fundamental behavior to be displayed both technically, in the job you are expected to do, and interpersonally, in how you relate to others. While most employers focus on technical competence, interpersonal competence is at least equally important. Interpersonal competence is our ability to demonstrate, "I've got your back," or the sense that you will be there in support of a colleague. This is precisely the type of competence that builds trust and reduces anxiety and stress.

4. *Concern.* Fiorina showed little concern for the 15,000 HP employees that would be laid off because of the Compaq merger, as well as the other employees who were laid off before and after that decision.

   Concern for employees begins with leaders making decisions that take employees into consideration. It continues through the culture by showing a genuine interest in what is going on in employees' lives. You don't need to know every detail, but I suggest that every supervisor should know one thing about the non-work lives of every one of their direct reports – and be able to discuss that one thing that is important to them on a weekly basis. This means that if you're interested in cars and your direct report is interested in underwater basket weaving, what will you discuss with that direct report? Underwater basket weaving. You discuss what is important to your direct report. I'm not suggesting doing therapy, speaking weekly for an hour. I'm suggesting five to fifteen minutes a week. This is how concern is demonstrated.

Taking Action

Every company will have strengths and weaknesses in building trust in one or more of these ROCC factors. Begin to discuss with your leadership team:

1. Which of these four factors (reliability, openness, competence, and concern) are strengths in your organization?
2. Which of these four factors are challenges in your organization?
3. What can you do in the next 30 days to begin to overcome your challenges?

CHAPTER 7

LANGUAGE

"Language is the road map of a culture. It tells you where
its people come from and where they are going."

- Rita Mae Brown,
Author

What You Need To Know:

1. Connectedness and trust are fundamental components of language development.

2. Language facilitates communication of complex concepts.

3. Every culture develops its own distinct language. Introducing a language into a culture is part of a cultural behavioral norm.

4. Language in a culture develops over time and should be a collaborative effort.

5. Culture must shift from the top down.

6. Language introductions must include both strategic and tactical steps.

Once you have established connectedness and trust in your organization, you have the opportunity to create a shared common language that both builds upon and reinforces these fundamental elements.

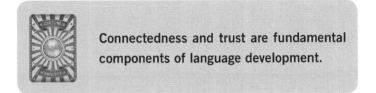

Connectedness and trust are fundamental components of language development.

Language is the sharing of specific symbols, sounds, or words to convey a specific meaning, procedure, complex concept, or construct. A shared common language is key to improving many systems. A shared common language increases business activity, profit, and efficiency – as well as connectedness and trust.

Organizations have made tremendous progress in recent years towards improving the development of a shared common language. Shared languages have increased organizational fortunes. Private and social interests are closely linked as the development of a shared language is a public, as well as a private, good. This public-private partnership is one reason why such progress has been made in both business and society.

A shared common language has also been found to dramatically increase bilateral trade between countries that speak the same language (for example, Spanish) by more than 40% – and bilateral investment by a factor of three or more.[1] By contrast, in Iceland, as much as 3% of annual GDP is, quite literally, "lost in translation" as a result of having to translate international, trade-related information into and out of Icelandic (which no other country speaks).[2]

To understand the benefits of a shared common language, we need only look as far as two well-known industrial networks over recent years: product supply chains and the World Wide Web. For both networks, a shared common language was the fundamental driver behind their transformation. In both cases, this transformation has delivered huge improvements in system resilience, productivity, efficiency, and profit.

Supply Chains

June 26, 1974. Recognize the date? No?

On that date, Clyde Dawson bought a 10-pack of Wrigley's Juicy Fruit chewing gum from a cashier named Sharon Buchanan at the Marsh Supermarket in Troy, Ohio. It rang up at 67 cents. It was the first time a barcode was scanned for a purchase – and the beginning of a revolution in the world of supply chains.

Over the past forty years, barcodes have become an easily recognizable, shared global language. Before barcodes, different, individually customized languages were used by suppliers, manufacturers, and retailers to inventory their products. This created huge inefficiencies as goods and products were recorded and re-recorded in different languages. It also created confusion, as there was no simple means of understanding and communicating along the supply chain.

In the early 1970s, members of the Grocery Manufacturers of America (GMA) decided they had had enough of the costly inefficiencies associated with translations. They created the Uniform Product Code (UPC), a shared common language, for recording the identity of specific products. The UPC was launched in 1974, initially for retail products, using barcode technology. It was an immediate success. By 1977, the UPC had become a shared global language for all products.

 Language facilitates communication of complex concepts.

During the 1980s and 1990s, this UPC technology began to reach different areas along the supply chain. A significant modification occurred in 1980, when a system was created for locating products, as well as identifying them. This system is referred to as the Global Location Number (GLN). The GLN ties products to fixed locations. Finally, in

1989, the Serial Shipping Container Code (SSCC) was created, enabling products to be grouped in transit.

These common data are a type of shared common language. It was this shared common language that provided, for the first time ever, a clear picture of the global supply chain. It created an end-to-end map from production, to distribution, to sale. This shared common language transformed production processes. Invoicing, purchase orders, distribution, and sales could now be easily shared across organizations in the new, shared common language.

Because the language of individual countries was no longer an obstacle to trade, the shared common language of UPCs, GLNs, and SSCCs helped to not only expand existing global supply links but create new ones as well. From the 1980s onward, supply chains expanded and strengthened across geographic boundaries; they became genuinely global. Between 1980 and 2010, the total value of world exports quintupled.[3]

This shared common language has continued to grow with the needs of those that use the language. In 2004, Global Data Synchronization Network (GDSN) became a shared common language that could be used for product descriptions with over 1,500 attributes, such as width, depth and height. Products can now be recorded in a consistent way globally, thanks to a shared common language. At a stroke, a unique "DNA string" was devised for each global product, describing its genetic makeup.

With an emerging language of product identifiers, locators, and attributes, the stage was set for an umbrella organization to maintain and develop these shared common languages. In 2005, this umbrella organization was created in the form of GS1. It is a global not-for-profit organization. GS1 currently has over 1.5 million members and maintains information on over 40 million products in its global registry. Like any language, it is an evolving, expanding, adapting genetic codebook for the global supply chain. A shared common language was the reason for the growth and success of the global supply chain.

World Wide Web

On October 29, 1969, the first-ever message was sent between computer networks. The message – sent between UCLA and Stanford University – was only five characters long ("login"). The system crashed at the letter "g." This was the inauspicious start to a technological revolution that would later be known as the World Wide Web. By the end of 1969, a network of campus computers was created – a nascent Internet.

In the early 1970s, the United States Defense Department's Advanced Research Projects Agency (DARPA) developed a network with electronic mail capabilities. In 1979, Compuserve made electronic mail available to a growing number of personal computer users. That same year, two graduate students at Duke University, Tom Truscott and Jim Ellis, developed Usenet. This was an early form of Internet forums, allowing users to post messages.

In 1983, more than a decade after its inception, a universal Internet protocol was created and agreed upon. This became the shared common language that provided an infrastructure and set of common technical standards for this evolving communications network, but the language of the Internet remained technical and diffuse. That meant it largely remained the domain of computer experts, libraries, and universities.

In 1990, Tim Berners-Lee and Robert Cailliau, colleagues working together at CERN, the Geneva-based nuclear research lab, authored a paper proposing the development of a World Wide Web, with links between and within documents creating a web-like information network.[4] This was in contrast to the highly-siloed approach to information storage and search that was the norm at the time. At the center of this web was a shared common language: Hyper-Text Markup Language (HTML). This allowed computers to communicate irrespective of their operating systems and underlying technologies.

To accompany this new language, Berners-Lee created some new location identifiers for this global web: Universal Resource Identifiers, the most well-known of which is the URL (Uniform Resource Locator). These were unique character strings for identifying web locations.

With a shared common language, common locators and an agreed syntax, the fundamental conditions were created for the web to spread worldwide, just as Berners-Lee had originally envisioned.

Success was not immediate. In June of 1993, there were still only 130 websites. But as web browsers became more accessible and available for home use, the web began to spread exponentially. By 1996, over 15 million users were surfing 100,000 websites. As of January, 2014, there were 2.5 billion Internet users worldwide, 834 million websites, and 244 billion emails sent daily.[5] None of this would have been possible without a shared common language. Like all successful languages, HTML has continued to adapt and change to meet changing demands. As of early 2014, HTML5 is the most current version being used.

With all shared common languages, there is an organization that monitors and tracks changes, as well as maintains the standard. Since 1994, the evolution and the maintenance of web standards have been overseen by a global organization called the World Wide Web Consortium (W3C). W3C (like GS1 for supply chains) is a not-for-profit organization. As of January 6, 2014, the W3C has 400 members from around the world.

The histories of the global supply chain and the Internet demonstrate the power of a shared common language to increase profit, efficiency, and connectedness – but how, exactly, are these outcomes achieved? To understand the processes underlying these gains, we must first understand the mechanics of language acquisition.

Language Acquisition

Children, over an extended period of time in a population of relatively homogenous language users, generally do learn language. This is a fact that follows from the general nature of our species and social organization. There is a great deal of empirical evidence that children, in particular, naturally accommodate new words. This suggests that the language acquisition process requires the learner to assume that words have distinct and contrasting meanings, and children use this process to understand objects, events, and their association to the word being used.

According to Eve V. Clark, a linguistics professor at Stanford University, the principles of human language acquisition in children follow a set of rules:[6]

1. Children rely on contrasting words to improve their understanding of semantics (the meaning of those words).
2. Children assume that new words contrast with those that they already know.
3. Children reject words they understand to be synonyms with terms that they already know.
4. Children generate novel words to fill expressive needs, but these new words tend to move towards traditional words and usage as their language development proceeds.

From another study, Clark provides empirical evidence that natural language acquisition exhibits two consistent principles:[7]

1. *The Principle of Contrast.* Every two consecutive words contrast in meaning.
2. *The Principle of Conventionality.* For certain meanings, there is a conventional word that speakers expect to be used in the language community.

These principles lead to systems of language that are efficient (all consecutive words contrast in meaning) and conservative (established words have priority).[8] This means that innovative words fill gaps in meaning as opposed to replacing established words with ones that have identical meanings.

To create a "language community" or a shared common language within a culture, we must understand the following features:

- Shared words within the language community must emphasize differences in semantics.
- Innovative or new words arise as a failure of the existing language to convey the desired or accurate meaning.
- New words, even if they are unusual, will be maintained and become a part of the shared common language if used with regularity to express a specific meaning.

Language, Culture, and the "Family"

A particularly colorful example of a language community exists within Mafia culture. I developed a reasonably robust understanding of this language community during the four years I spent working as a psychologist in the Federal Bureau of Prisons.

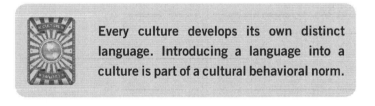

Every culture develops its own distinct language. Introducing a language into a culture is part of a cultural behavioral norm.

Language as a part of culture develops similarly in both illegal and legal organizations. As with any other culture, language is developed over time to increase understanding and trust. Some of the more interesting and expressive Mafia idioms I encountered include:

a friend of mine: an introduction of a third person who is not a member of the Family, but who can be vouched for by a Family member

a friend of ours: an introduction of one made man to another made man

associate: one who works with mobsters, but hasn't been asked to take the vow of *Omertá* (vow of silence; if broken it is punishable by death); an almost-made man *the books*: a phrase indicating potential promotion in the Family; can be open or closed depending on possibility for promotion

clip: to murder; also referred to as "break an egg," "burn," "do a piece of work," "hit," "ice," "pop," "put out a contract on," and "whack"

capo: the Family member who leads a crew; short for *capodecina*

come heavy: to walk in carrying a loaded gun

cugine: a young "soldier" striving to be "made"

made man: an indoctrinated member of the Family. Essentially, you pledge your allegiance to the boss and the family for life. To even qualify, your mother has to be Italian.

Moe Green Special: Getting killed with a shot in the eye, like the character, Moe Green, in *The Godfather*; one form of "sending a message"

soldier: the bottom-level member of an organized crime Family; also "foot soldier"

wise guy: a made man

Developing Language in a Culture

A shared common language is a prerequisite for collaboration and trust. Without a shared language, meaningful collaboration is impossible and trust becomes extremely difficult to establish.

So, how does a shared common language actually develop? Research indicates that shared language development occurs through both formal and informal training and usage.[9] These formal and informal structures should be considered in the creation of any shared language.

Whether the shared common language in a culture is already established, or the shared common language is shifting, or new people are being introduced to the shared common language, there are two preparation steps to either establishing or enhancing a successful shared common language.

The first step is to set expectations. This means that everyone involved in the process of developing a shared common language must understand that language acquisition and development happens over time. Members of the culture, new and established, should be given time to learn the words and meanings of the shared common language. Organizations hoping to reap the benefits of a shared common language should not allow individual frustration and impatience to "short cut" the shared language development process. It is necessary to create a foundation of collaboration and trust, and this takes time.

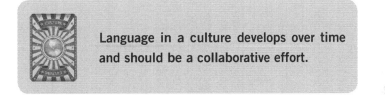

Language in a culture develops over time and should be a collaborative effort.

The second step to creating a shared common language, whether virtually or face-to-face, is to create time and space for its development. This is particularly necessary when introducing new members to the culture, but also important when putting together new teams that come from different work environments.

For many people, this two-step preparation process would seem to necessitate the creation of a dictionary of shared terms. Although having a dictionary of terms in one's culture is one way to codify a shared language, it is certainly not the only way.

With or without a dictionary, there are three approaches to creating the type of interactions that develop and facilitate a shared common language:

1. *Learn your group and culture.* Members' personal and professional backgrounds, history, worldviews, and values comprise a culture. Keep in mind that people with different backgrounds are likely to use words differently. Shared language doesn't require everyone to use precisely the same terms; it requires

simply understanding the meaning of those terms and how they are being used.

2. *Facilitate term-gap identification.* This is a key component of creating a shared common language. When people discuss concepts, processes, procedures, desires, and goals related to the culture, they will often do so in terms from their own background and experience. It is during this time that a gap in terms can be identified and clarification can be requested and offered. This process of discussion, which begins with a gap in terms, requires people to stretch their minds to understand the perspective of others. It is in this understanding that a shared common language is developed.

3. *Create and protect time and space where the development of a shared common language is the primary goal.* While some shared common language will develop informally and spontaneously, time and space are necessary to expand the reach of a shared common language. Treat shared common language as a living, breathing entity that will continue to grow and morph. If you try to lock it down, it will lead to frustration and stress on the part of the people using the language.

Developing a shared common language will always be a "work in progress." Having employees work together in the same context and culture is a wonderful way to develop a shared common language – and, ultimately, stronger and more efficient relationships. When people within a culture understand the subtle meaning of specific phrases and terms, they can build trust in one another and in the culture, and focus on the work that needs to get done rather than feeling like they need to be constantly walking on eggshells.

DPS Telecom

Culture starts at the top of an organization, and, like water, flows down through the organization, even to the lowest points and hidden corners. When culture is made part of a broad strategy, and has specific tactical steps yoked to that strategy, behavioral norms change. A powerful example of shared common language in action is the cultural transformation story of DPS Telecom.

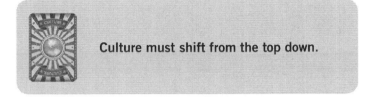

Culture must shift from the top down.

DPS Telecom builds customized network reliability solutions made to their clients' specifications. They are a high-mix, low-volume producer of remote site-monitoring systems. Customization is a key component of their products.

Between 2008 and 2013, DPS Telecom grew from $6M to $13M in sales and went from 13% pre-tax profit to greater than 45% pre-tax profit. Its CEO would tell you these changes came in large part due to a cultural shift, which was set in motion by the development of a shared common language. Prior to this cultural shift, DPS struggled to keep new employees past the one-year mark. Now, more than 50% of employees have been with DPS Telecom for five years or more.

The CEO and founder of DPS systems is an exceedingly bright, hard-working, and "righteous dude" (he's got the staff surveys to prove exactly that) named Robert (Bob) Berry. Bob is a big promoter of using business modeling to successfully grow his company. Business modeling is not a new technique or system; it has been around for years. What *is* new is how Bob was able to apply this technique to change the culture at DPS Telecom.

The DPS Culture Shift

The company's toxic culture became painfully clear at DPS when they began to create standard operating procedures (SOPs) and best practices for all key positions. The result? Drama! The behaviors they saw among employees are well-known to anyone who has ever undergone a cultural shift or worked in a weak culture: excuses, missed deadlines, infighting, poor attendance and participation, and staff turnover. All these behaviors are par for the course when a culture is going from having poor or no metrics for performance to a culture with strong metrics for performance. In this case, the process of documenting SOPs was clearly going to create some very specific metrics. Employees who were accustomed to performing poorly without consequences were going to lose that freedom, and – not surprisingly - they resisted the push for process documentation and metrics.

At the heart of this resistance was found to be a very specific type of employee: the "MTM." An MTM employee was one who tried to "Manage the Manager." This simple acronym served as a shorthand for communicating a complex construct and is just one example of the language that DPS developed.

Specifically, an MTM employee was one who exhibited several of these behaviors:

- Couldn't do the job but had great social skills to cover up that fact
- Seemed full of promise but didn't believe the job was right for them
- Always had excuses for poor performance
- Tended to "hoard" information
- Threatened to quit with some frequency if pressured to perform
- Performance wouldn't improve, and it was always the fault of the training or the coach
- Tended to "infect" others with their discontent

The "DPSisms" – or shared common language that developed through the specific focus on culture – played a significant role in the cultural shift at the company. This is language that everyone at DPS understands simply by hearing the phrase. In addition to "MTM," other powerful phrases and terms emerged, including:

- *Fail fast.* Periodic failure is expected, and it is a point best reached quickly. Failing quickly shortens the learning curve and allows less time and energy to be invested into the path that leads to failure.
- *The first time sucks the most (... the second time sucks a little less; the third time a little less still; by the fourth time you're getting an idea of how it's supposed to work).* Improving a process takes time and repetition. Don't be afraid to try new things and don't expect it to go well or be easy the first time out of the gate.
- *Make it your fault.* Find the place that you have responsibility in the process. Don't push off responsibility (or blame) onto others. You have no control over the other people in the world, only your own thoughts, words, and deeds. If something goes wrong, and you say that you can go no further until "they" fix their piece, then you have completely undermined your own ability to take control of the situation. Keep your influence in the situation.
- *If we don't take care of the client, someone else will.* The importance of customer service and responsiveness can never be overstated.
- *Focus on the results, not the work.* Remember the importance of metrics in the culture. You do what is necessary (within the guidelines of what is legal and ethical) to meet the desired results.

The development of this shared common language allowed the management team at DPS to do two critical things: (1) codify and better understand the problematic elements of their existing culture that needed to change; and (2) identify the new elements of the future, more successful culture they wanted to cultivate.

Language introductions must include both strategic and tactical steps.

In response to this new understanding, the management team at DPS came together to begin the transformation of their culture. Several strategic decisions were made in order to create a cultural shift:

- No drama (undue or unnecessary emotion) would be permitted in the organization.
- If employees did not fit or could not flex to the cultural rules, an exit would be facilitated.
- Job knowledge and information would be shared broadly.
- All positions would have at least three people in the company who could do that job.
- A special effort would be made to retain employees with more than one year of experience.

The specific tactical steps that were implemented as a result of these strategies included:

- MTMs would be "set free" to pursue other interests – quickly.
- Company-wide luncheons were held on a monthly basis. This allowed the leadership to share information broadly, undermining any MTM misinformation or rumors that so often created employee dissatisfaction. These meetings also proved to be critical to building common vocabulary between staff and management around goals and concepts.
- SOPs were completed and cross-training executed for every function in the organization.
- Quarterly bonuses were tied to metrics that became much easier to determine through the development of SOPs.

- The recruiting process would focus on existing skills, ability to learn new skills, and "goodness of fit" into DPS culture.

The results of the strategic and tactical changes focused on culture – and initiated by the development of a shared common language – were astonishing. Five years after initiating the cultural shift and its policies, the culture is one that everyone enjoys. Even more impressive is the fact that, during the transformation period, DPS Telecom more than doubled its sales and more than tripled its pre-tax profitability.

So What?

Language is just one part of a cultural shift. When language is a critical focus of culture, members of the organization begin to trust one another and understand complex concepts in a linguistic "short hand" so more gets accomplished in less time.

Taking Action

1. What are some of the common terms or phrases used in your culture?
2. What are some of the misunderstandings that occur and recur because of the lack of a common language?
3. What are some of the complex concepts in your company that would lend themselves to a shared common language?
4. What are your next steps to ensuring a language in your culture that connects people through communication?

CHAPTER 8

TIME PERSPECTIVE

"Time is what we want most, but what we use worst."

– William Penn,
Founder of Pennsylvania

What You Need to Know:

1. The present is now, real, and concrete. The past and future are abstractions. They do not exist other than how they are created in our minds.

2. A person's ability to delay gratification, even at four years of age, may predict many future outcomes.

3. People who don't have the capacity for future orientation as children have difficulty understanding if-then relationships, causal relationships, and probabilities.

4. Reliability of the people in his or her world allows a child to develop the ability to delay gratification and develop a future orientation.

5. Children's brains today are being "wired" differently than those of people from earlier generations.

6. Time perspective exerts a profound influence on human behavior, but people are often unaware of its effects. All time perspectives have positive and negative qualities. At their extremes, the negatives outweigh the positives.

Life is about choices. We are faced with choices, small and large, every day. Do I go to work or play? Do I study or go out with friends? Do I eat more or stop eating now? How many drinks do I have before driving? Do I dive into that chocolate even though I'm a diabetic?

For many of the choices that confront us, the underlying choice is between giving in to temptation versus delaying gratification.

This is the fundamental question that is informed by our time perspective. This is also the question that is faced by our family members, coworkers, colleagues, and employees. Time perspective is highly influenced by our culture and environment, beginning as early as age four.

Human beings divide their experience into different time perspectives, generally without thinking about it – or even being aware of it. These perspectives vary between cultures, social classes, and individuals. People become biased by over-relying on some time perspectives and essentially ignoring others. Time perspective is one of the most powerful influences on human behavior on an individual, group, organization, and even national level.

> The present is now, real, and concrete. The past and future are abstractions. They do not exist other than how they are created in our minds.

Philip Zimbardo, a psychologist at Stanford University, has been studying time and the human experience of time (time perspective) for more than thirty years. What he and his team discovered is that, while our language only offers us three periods of time (past, present and future), the human experience of time is more complex. For example, Zimbardo has found that each of the time periods articulated by our language is divided into two variations. So, the past has two forms, the present has two forms, and the future has two forms – for a total of six unique time perspectives.[1]

How we use – or fail to use – each of these time perspectives helps to explain the decisions that people make as members of an organization or society. As an example, this chapter will illustrate how the behaviors we see at the tender age of four can explain some of the behaviors that led to the financial meltdown of 2008.

The Original Marshmallow Experiment

In the late 1960s and early 1970s, psychologist Walter Mischel did an experiment that later became known as "The Marshmallow Experiment."[2] He brought four-year-old preschoolers into a room and created an emotional cognitive dilemma.

After sitting a child down at a table, he put a single marshmallow on the table in front of the child. He then said that he had to step out of the room for a few minutes and explained to the child that she or he could eat the one marshmallow on the table now – or, if they waited to eat it until he returned, they could get a second marshmallow. So, the choice was either one marshmallow now (immediate gratification) or two marshmallows later (delayed gratification).

 A person's ability to delay gratification, even at four years of age, may predict many future outcomes.

The children's behavior revealed all sorts of information. Is a bird in the hand worth two in the bush? Is the child's behavior at this point in time impulsive or reflective? It also revealed what Zimbardo refers to as present-oriented versus future-oriented time perspective.

The past and future are abstractions. They do not exist other than how they are created in our minds. They are not places you can see, taste, or visit. By contrast, the present is now, real, and concrete. It has empirical reality.

We are all born into the present time perspective. Beginning at birth, we seek to obtain pleasure through food and cuddling – and to avoid pain. Through our environment (society, education, culture, etc.), we learn to build additional time perspectives. The first alternative time perspective we learn is future orientation.

Future-oriented time perspective means we can imagine a future that does not yet exist, but may exist based on our actions. If the imagined future seems both better than current reality and reasonably possible, we're willing to (a) work towards it and (b) forgo current small rewards in expectation of larger potential rewards later. By contrast, people who are exclusively present-oriented fail to see the value of holding out for potentially "more later" and instead tend to choose "what is certain now" (emphasis on the *now*) – even if it's less.

 People who don't have the capacity for future orientation as children have difficulty understanding if-then relationships, causal relationships, and probabilities.

Thanks to Mischel's original marshmallow experiment and other related work, we have learned that people who don't have the capacity for future orientation as children have difficulty understanding if-then relationships, causal relationships, and probabilities. If they have difficulty learning this, they have difficulty making long-term decisions in life, because life is about choices, probability assessment, if-then conditions, and causal relationships within those choices.

Here's what we know: before the age of four, no child can wait for the second marshmallow. Delaying gratification, a behavior tied to future orientation, requires the development of certain parts of the brain that do not develop before the age of four. At four years of age, about 50% of children can wait, and as they get even older, more of them are able to delay gratification. This future orientation develops as a result of socialization, education, and culture.

Part of the uniqueness and beauty of Mischel's experiment was that he was able to follow up with the same children fourteen years later. He obtained their school records, interviewed their parents, and interviewed the original children, who were then eighteen years old.

There were enormous differences between the children who at four years old were present-oriented compared to those who were future-oriented. The children who had been present-oriented at four years old (who had immediately gobbled up the single marshmallow) had grown into young adults who were:

- Moody
- Easily frustrated
- Indecisive
- Prone to jealousy and envy

By contrast, the children who at four years old had been future-oriented (able to hold out for the second marshmallow) had become young adults who:

- Scored 250 points higher on their SAT tests
- Were cooperative
- Worked well under pressure
- Were confident and self-reliant

Clearly, a person's ability to delay gratification (develop and apply future orientation), even at age four, can predict many future outcomes. However, *this is not genetic*. These are *not* personality factors. These are *learned behaviors* that involve many environmental and cultural factors. Environmental factors include: culture, geography, religion, social class, educational level, political and economic stability, family, friends, society, age, and gender. Even climate and geography play a role. If your climate remains relatively stable year-round, there's less need for you to develop the ability to prepare for a future that is significantly different from the present. So, for example, the closer you live to the equator (where climate is relatively consistent), the more present-oriented you tend to be.

Knowing the cultural factors that impact time perspective, we have the ability to create a culture that can influence our own time perspective. When we create a culture that supports our desired time perspective, we can teach and help those around us function within that time perspective.

Updated Marshmallow Experiment

But wait ... there's more. In a study done at the University of Rochester and published in the journal *Cognition* in January of 2013, Celeste Kidd, Holly Palmeri, and Richard Aslin reran the Mischel experiment with a slight twist.[3]

They divided the children into two groups. Before the actual marshmallow test was conducted, one group of children was given a broken promise. These children were told that the experimenter would bring them additional supplics to do an art project if they waited for them, but the experimenter never brought them the art supplies, even after the child had waited. This was the "unreliable tester" group.

The second group of children experienced a fulfilled promise prior to their marshmallow test. In this condition, the experimenter actually *did* bring additional art supplies, as promised. This was the "reliable tester" group.

Once it was time for the actual marshmallow test (eat one now or hold out for two later), the children in the reliable tester group waited up to four times longer (twelve minutes) than the children in the unreliable tester group. The authors argue that this calls into question any interpretation that impulsivity in childhood is based on personality or character. The authors suggest that in order for the correlations between marshmallow performance and later-life success to be valid, one must consider the environment in which the children were raised, not just from before age four, but all the way up to age eighteen.

 Reliability of the people in his or her world allows a child to develop the ability to delay gratification and develop a future orientation.

Specifically, while many have (mis)interpreted Walter Mischel's results to mean that impulsivity versus the ability to delay gratification at age four reflects stable character or personality traits, it's important to remember that culture trumps personality. As Zimbardo suggests, present-orientated versus future-orientated time perspective is developed (and flexible) based on environment and/or culture.

Moreover, Kidd, Palmeri, and Aslin discovered that it is the specific factor of *reliability* that allows children to develop the ability to delay gratification and develop a future orientation. Children are processing information about their environment even at the age of four. If the environment that the child has experienced only rarely provides long-term gain, then it makes perfect sense for the child to behave impulsively. It will maximize their reward in the least time, and there is no reward for waiting. The child must believe or trust that there will be a reward for delaying gratification; that's how future-oriented time perspective is developed.

To be future-oriented, you must have *trust* in the promises that people make and in your ability to modify the future through your own behavior. This means that you (or your child or employee) need a relatively stable family life, work environment, political life, and economic life. If you live in a country with 1000% inflation, like Zimbabwe or Argentina have had in the recent past, you don't save for a rainy day. You spend what you have today because you don't trust that the currency you hold will be worth as much tomorrow.

Understanding our own tendencies regarding time perspective can show us our own strengths and weaknesses when it comes to time and help us understand the perspective of others.

The Six Time Perspectives

As mentioned earlier, we all begin life as present-oriented beings. Over time, we learn language that teaches us three time orientations (past, present, and future). Culture, society, education, and experiences move us to be more past-oriented or future-oriented.

Zimbardo determined that each of our linguistic time perspectives is further broken down into two time perspectives.[4] These are:

1. Past positive
2. Past negative
3. Present gratification
4. Present fatalism
5. Future goal
6. Future transcendental

Past Positive. This time perspective is experienced when one's focus is on positive memories of the past. There are frequent references to "the good old days," a tendency to hold on to objects from the past (old photos, books, report cards, etc.) and a general tendency towards nostalgia. In cultures that are preliterate, there is always a storyteller who is responsible for delivering positive memories. The storyteller's job is to keep the past alive. These are almost always stories that glorify their ancestors and give children a sense of reverence for their elders and ancestors. Such stories also serve to instill in children a sense of connection to the past and present community, with the hope that they will follow in the footsteps of their parents and grandparents, and remain in the community.

Past Negative. This time perspective occurs when one's focus is on negative memories of the past. This can occur either when people have had genuinely negative experiences or when they simply remember the past inaccurately in a negative way. Wars are often fought because of the past being brought into the present (Sunni vs. Shia, United States Civil War, etc.). People stuck in a past negative time perspective are easily identified, as they are often trapped in cycle of negativity. In some cases, if you know them well enough, you can see that their thinking is ruminative or obsessive. They do not have the ability to see the future as potentially being different (and better than) the past. This is also the foundation of clinical depression. A person stuck in a past negative time perspective always ruminates on past negative (real or perceived) events. Getting stuck in this time frame, or developing a bias towards it, always creates negative outcomes.

Present Gratification. What Zimbardo referred to as present hedonism, I refer to as present gratification. We all begin our lives with a present gratification time perspective. Whether we were fed from our mother's breast or a bottle, we all start our lives in present gratification, seeking pleasure in the short term and avoiding pain.

This is the time perspective when one's focus is on the here and now, with good friends and social connections. People who get stuck within this time frame often succumb easily to temptation. People who get stuck here never have a "to do" list. They don't need one because they only think about the present, not the future. They don't think about the future because their only concern is what's going on now, and are susceptible to addictions such as drugs, alcohol, and gambling.

The problem with getting stuck in or developing a bias for present gratification perspective is that your behavior is never guided by imagined future consequences or "the shadow of the future." Your behavior is only influenced by the immediate circumstances of the situation. For people unable to flex beyond this time frame, friends are their most important assets. These are the people who spend their time making friends and maintaining friendships. They arrive at parties early and stay late, and they are always the ones who are last to leave. They never worry about tomorrow ... they just don't want to miss anything *now*!

Casinos are a great example of an environment created specifically to draw in those who have a bias towards present gratification. You don't have to walk far into one to realize there are no clocks or windows – nothing to give gamblers any indication that time is passing. Time stands still in a casino. Casinos are a trap for anyone who has tendencies towards present gratification.

Video games are another powerful example of the allure – and danger – of a present gratification perspective. Video games create a self-contained environment where the constantly changing visual stimulation creates a high level of excitement that traps people in the present moment. In the US, by the time an average boy is twenty-one years old, he has spent 10,000 hours playing video games alone.[5] It takes 10,000 hours to develop expertise in anything, regardless of initial level of talent.[6] This is the equivalent of more than five years at a full-time job playing video games. This fact fuels the concern that many of these young people will also have challenges with their social skills and emotional and social intelligence.

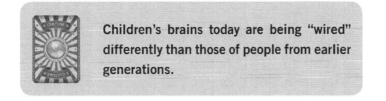

Children's brains today are being "wired" differently than those of people from earlier generations.

In fact, the brains of today's children are being "wired" differently than those of people from earlier generations.[7] They have grown up in a digital world where they can control images in front of them and the world around them. This means they may struggle to function well in a traditional classroom or workplace that is "analog" (rather than digital or computer-generated). For these children, "real" environments are static, boring, and uncontrollable. As students (or future employees), they are expected to be passive, merely taking in and processing information or engaging in what to them feel like mindless tasks.

Present Fatalism. People with this time perspective believe that it doesn't pay to plan because they believe "nothing works out for me." Those with a bias towards this time perspective believe that life is predestined. Life is controlled by fate, by God, by my boss, or by my company – all of whom are stacking the deck against me. These can also be seen as the people who just "give up."

People who live in poverty get stuck in a present fatalistic time perspective. For them, it is a realistic, rational time perspective. If you are poor, your life is often controlled by factors, events, or people outside of your influence. Much of your planning is stifled and doesn't lead to anything constructive. Unfortunately, once you internalize or create a bias for this time perspective, a self-fulfilling prophecy dooms you to remain in poverty. If you believe that effort and planning can't or won't change anything about your future, then you don't make the effort and/ or plan. The person in poverty might say, "It doesn't pay to get educated – it's a lot of effort and it won't change anything," or "It doesn't pay to work – I'd be last hired and the first fired." As a society, when we have institutions and systems that fail to teach and reward people to plan, we find ourselves with larger and larger numbers of people "giving up" and remaining in poverty.

Poverty is not genetic. It exists and persists for multiple generations because children who are born into poverty and grow up in poverty too often learn a present fatalistic time perspective from their parents and their situation. As a result, they are often not afforded opportunities to learn future time perspectives. When this time perspective is transferred from parent to child, generations of the same family remain in poverty. Children who grow up in poverty grow up in a present gratification or present fatalistic world, unless they are exposed to someone or something, such as education, which can teach them a future time perspective.

In business, people with a present fatalistic time perspective are employees who tend to be the consistent naysayers within a group. They will find reasons that new concepts or initiatives won't work, and they try to get others to align with their perspective. They see no reason to try new things if the outcome is predetermined by the obstacles they've already identified.

Future Goal. This is the time perspective where people focus less on current aspects of their lives and more on their anticipated, desired, abstract vision of the future. They focus on the outcomes of different potential options, given their current circumstances. They develop strengths in logical analysis, if-then reasoning, probable outcomes, and tracking the steps necessary to get from start to finish. Many successful, high-achieving people are masters of this time perspective, being both able to recognize if-then conditions and accurately project consequences.

When people focus on this time perspective, they have a concern for the consequences of their actions. They focus on responsibility and achieving the best outcomes. They delay gratification and resist temptations more easily. They are prepared to invest effort and resources now, as long as they see there will be a payoff, even if it is in the distant future, often enduring unpleasant situations in the present for the promise of better future outcomes.

People with a tendency towards this time perspective tend not to take physical risks. They tend to be conscientious, health-conscious, and engage in a variety of behaviors that improve long-term health, even if they require time, effort, and money (flossing, taking vitamins, eating healthy foods, getting regular health checkups, etc.). They make these investments even if there is little perceptible immediate gain because they believe that they are investing in the prevention of future adverse health events.

Physical therapists' offices offer a great example of human variation in time perspectives. In the United States, half of all people who start with physical therapy (for any reason) never finish.[8] Why? Because all physical therapy makes things feel worse – at first. So, a lot of people quit. The ones that quit are present-oriented and past-oriented. By contrast, future-oriented people have a future scenario in mind where they will be well again, so they stick it out and push past the initial pain and discomfort – and, as a result, actually do get better.

Although the future-oriented time perspective offers a generally healthy and adaptive approach to life, it is not entirely without its down side. People who get stuck in a future-oriented time perspective are often unable to enjoy activities or experiences in the present. They tend to look at present activities that don't have a future-oriented goal as a "waste of time." Emotional intimacy can be a challenge for people who develop a bias for this time perspective. They have difficulty with spontaneity, things they cannot control, and things that don't appear to advance them towards some desired future goal.

In business, you will often find companies are overstocked with executives with a future-oriented time perspective bias. They are always seeking to get more done in less time. However, if they are unable to achieve as much as they desire, they will often experience high levels of anxiety and workaholism. Moreover, this pattern of work can often lead to high levels of early achievement that later can leave people with a sense that all the work wasn't worth it or wasn't actually meaningful. Now that the goal is achieved, what is its meaning? This is a recipe for a mid-life or late-life crisis.

Future Transcendental. This time perspective is not often taught or widely understood in the United States, but it is seen among many religious groups. This time frame instills the focus on life after death of the mortal body. This time frame is particularly prevalent among Puritans, Calvinists, Protestants, Catholics, and Muslims. Many people who are steeped in these religions spend their whole lives preparing to go to heaven (and trying to avoid going to hell or its equivalent).

Holistic Expanded Present. Although it was not part of Zimbardo's original model, data has recently begun to be collected on a seventh type of time perspective, which is currently less defined than the original six.[9] This additional time perspective is being referred to as the "holistic expanded present." In this time perspective, people are focused on experiencing the "now" while also doing what they see as right for the future, without being attached to the outcome. This means that they focus on the present in the service of the future, but can remain detached from whatever result may occur. This time frame can be learned, and it is taught through Zen, Buddhism, Yoga Science, and other Eastern philosophies. The tool or skill that is most used to teach this time perspective is meditation. Meditation focuses on being able to still the brain and be in the present moment, while also bringing the past and the future into that moment. This concept is understandably difficult to measure, but its philosophy can be seen in the Sanskrit saying, "Yesterday is already a dream and tomorrow only a vision, but today, well lived, makes every yesterday a dream of happiness and every tomorrow a vision of hope."

Time perspective exerts a profound influence on human behavior, but people are often unaware of its effects. All time perspectives have positive and negative qualities. At their extremes, the negatives outweigh the positives.

Different time perspectives clearly show us that the time perspectives we apply have a tremendous influence on us, the people around us, and the organizations to which we belong. When we better understand how each perspective develops, we have a better understanding of how each time perspective acts upon us. This is how we can begin to shape our future.

The table below illustrates both the positive and negative qualities of each time perspective. At their extremes, the negatives outweigh the positives – and, as a result, it means that getting stuck in any one of these time perspectives has deleterious effects.

	Positive Components	Negative Components
Past Perspective	Happiness, self-esteem, patriotism, gratitude, wisdom, family values, personal identity stemming from connection with the past	Trauma, guilt, depression, retaliation, revenge, resistance to change
Present Perspective	High affiliation, joy in life, sensuality, sexuality, energy/activity, improvisation, search for novelty/innovation	Addiction-prone, risk-seeking, violent, angry, reliant on luck rather than effort, prone to gambling/credit card debt
Future Perspective	High achievement, high self-efficacy, health-focused, probabilistic thinking, cost-benefit analysis, optimistic	Anxiety, worry, social isolation, competitiveness, sexual impotence

Figure 1: The positive and negative qualities of
the three linguistic time perspectives.

The best strategy is to understand and be able to flex between time perspectives — to be able to apply the best one to any given circumstance, in pursuit of your happiness and success.

The Dangers of Present-Time Perspectives

As illustrated in the previous table, all time perspectives have their strengths and weaknesses, the latter of which are particularly apparent when a time perspective is taken to extremes.

The contrast between the "light" and "dark" sides of time perspectives is especially stark for present-oriented time perspectives, and many of history's most significant debacles can be traced to an excess of the "dark" side of this perspective.

At the individual level, an obsessive focus on present time perspective tends to manifest as exceedingly poor risk assessment, ultimately leading to very poor judgment. You will recognize these people as the ones who can't think two steps ahead. They tend to be surprised by circumstances that would be easily predictable to someone who was future-goal-oriented. They tend not to think of long-term consequences before making decisions, whether it is how to respond to a colleague or a long-term business decision. These types of people are often seen as a liability to a company, but we will see later in this section how their time perspective is necessary for creativity and relationship building.

Risk-taking behavior can manifest itself in many ways outside of the business environment as well, such as in risk-taking behaviors while driving. Studies have shown that although insurance companies tend to consider males as higher risk takers behind the wheel, it is actually time perspective that is the best predictor.[10] When you look at time perspectives, it's those with a bias towards a present gratification time perspective (whether male or female) that are more apt to take risks behind the wheel. These correlations hold true for speeding, drunk driving, racing, and wearing seatbelts. That being said, it's also possible that society socializes men to be more present-oriented than women, in which case gender and time orientation are conflated.

Addictions of all shapes and sizes are also a result of present orientation.[11] It is after multiple uses that you become psychologically and/or physically addicted and the negative consequences begin to affect you. For the present-oriented person, pleasure in the present is guaranteed. The future is merely probable. Not everyone who does drugs gets addicted, just like not everyone who smokes gets cancer — and it's easy for present-oriented people to convince themselves that since they feel just fine now, these negative consequences are things that "only happen to other people."

Present-Time Perspectives and the 2008 Financial Meltdown

The financial market meltdown in 2008 had all sorts of creativity in its underpinnings. Collateralized debt obligations (CDOs) were financial products that produced income *now*, in the present, rather than the conservative future orientation applied by previous generations of investment bankers. To further reward the present orientation, there were no negative consequences for those that sold these products ... only for those who bought them.

The financial meltdown was caused by a culture that demanded a present orientation motivated by creativity and a culture of greed. This time orientation in the financial world, as we have seen, has the capacity to transform usually wise and future-oriented business leaders and managers (who would ordinarily be more cautious) into present-oriented, hedonistic, short-term thinkers. Bankers behaved like exaggerated versions of the children in the marshmallow experiment. They searched out the experimenter's hidden stash of marshmallows and gorged themselves on them all, not caring about the future consequences (at least not for anyone else).

The Benefits of Present-Time Perspectives

With all of these potential pitfalls, it's worth asking if being present-oriented is *ever* good for *anything*. Yes, as it turns out, it definitely is. Case in point:

In an experiment comparing the creativity of people with present orientation versus future orientation,[12] subjects were given a task to do and were either told to focus on the *outcome* (being told that their performance would be evaluated on the outcome they achieved) or on the *process* (being told simply to do the best they could do) for each experimental task.

The natural tendency of present-oriented people is to focus on process; the natural tendency of future oriented-people is to focus on outcome. These were the results of the study:

- Present-oriented people were much more creative in *both* their process and outcomes.
- Present-oriented people did not like being in the future-oriented (outcome-oriented) condition.
- Future-oriented people performed well on measures of technical merit, but struggled in terms of creativity.

- All measures of creativity were dominated by present-oriented people.

Present-oriented people are better able to take something in the present and view it in a totally different way. They have no need to stick to a model of what the outcome should be. They don't look toward the future. They have no interest in doing things the way they've been done before. To them, that's boring. They don't care about the outcome being judged, they just want to do something different in the moment, simply for the sake of variety. This is where improvisation and innovation come from.

Creativity, spontaneity, and innovation are precisely the reasons why, in business, we want to create environments in our workplace where this type of thinking will take place. To be successful, we need to create cultures that allow for (and require) both present-oriented thinking in some situations and future-oriented thinking in other situations.

Optimal Temporal Balance

Time perspectives are not fixed. People will respond to the culture, environment, and situation by relying on the most effective time perspective for the situation – or the time perspective that is prevalent in that situation. So, in order to create the best environment for yourself, your family, and your colleagues and coworkers, it is important to develop the mental flexibility necessary to shift time perspective with ease. Consider that when you do this, you do this not only for yourself, but also for those around you. In the long run, if you are able to balance your time perspectives, your life will be happier, more fulfilling, longer, and more successful.[13]

Recognizing that the optimal time perspective is likely to vary by situation, is it nevertheless possible to identify a profile of the most broadly adaptive time perspective tendencies? Indeed it is. Based on Zimbardo's work, the most well-adjusted and high-performing people score well below average on measures of past negative and present fatalism, about average on measures of future transcendental, significantly above average on measures of present gratification and future goal, and off the charts on past positive.

Past perspectives give you roots and stability. They connect you to your historical identity and family and help keep you grounded. Future perspectives give you lift so that you can fly and overcome new challenges. Present perspectives give you energy to explore people, places and yourself. They keep important people close to you and give you the freedom to improvise and innovate.

If you're interested in better understanding your own time perspectives, you can access a *free* Time Perspective Assessment at www.thetimeparadox.com/surveys.[14] You can then compare your results to the graph below, which represents the results of Zimbardo's ongoing research in this space and provides an overview of the range of scores on each time perspective measurement.

Time Perspective

Percentage of People Who Share Your Score	Past Negative	Past Positive	Present Fatalism	Present Gratification	Future Goal	Future Transcendental
99%	4.7	4.11	3.89	4.65	4.15	4.80
90%	4.0	3.67	3.11	4.53	3.85	4.4
80%	3.7	3.56	2.78	4.33	3.69	4.10
70%	3.4	3.44	2.67	4.13	3.62	3.9
60%	3.2	3.33	2.44	4.00	3.54	3.60
50%	3.0	3.22	2.33	3.93	3.38	3.4
40%	2.8	3.11	2.22	3.80	3.31	3.20
30%	2.6	3.0	2.0	3.67	3.23	2.9
20%	2.4	2.78	1.89	3.47	3.08	2.50
10%	2.1	2.56	1.67	3.27	2.85	1.9
1%	1.4	2.00	1.11	2.67	2.31	1.40

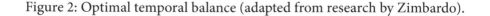 Optimal Temporal Balance

Figure 2: Optimal temporal balance (adapted from research by Zimbardo).

The dots and lines represent Zimbardo's idea of what an ideal time perspective looks like. Once you've taken the online assessment yourself, you can print out and plot your scores, connect the dots, and then see how your time perspective compares with that of others. This will also give you can have a better idea of your strengths and challenges regarding your own time perspectives.

Changing Your Time Perspective

Because all of us begin life as present-oriented beings, it is difficult to teach future perspectives, particularly to those born into or raised in poverty. The present is immediately gratifying, while the future requires delay of gratification as well as mental flexibility. It requires you to trust that the future can be as you would like it to be if you exert certain effort. This doesn't happen automatically; it takes training and practice.

Taking present-oriented people and turning them into future-goal-oriented people can be done through mental simulation. This technique is used by many professional athletes. They visualize not only success, but also the specific steps they need to go through to reach that success. This technique has also been shown to be effective in reforming the behavior of juvenile delinquents.

In 2010, psychologist Rueben Robbins took adolescents with behavior problems and taught them to practice mental simulation with goals at different temporal distances into the future.[15] First they started with goals they could achieve the next day, then two days, then three days, a week, a month, a year, and finally up to five years into future. Over two weeks of training, the ability to establish future orientation became much more concrete and pragmatic. They went from wanting to be doctors and lawyers (an unrealistic future goal if you're failing high school) to wanting to be able to go back to their regular high school or get their GED. They learned to reach for things that were both more tangible and more obtainable. For most of the kids in the study, it helped them achieve the most important thing of all, which was to maintain their freedom by staying out of jail. For the record, the study wasn't designed to crush young people's dreams; it was designed to help people learn to set realistic, progressive goals – and work to obtain them. Having obtained a first set of goals, they were then encouraged to set a second (then third, fourth and so on) set of goals – and know that they had the skills and experience to engage in the behaviors necessary to achieve those subsequent goals as well.

Robbins' study is a lesson for all of us. Through mental simulation strategies, we can help people become more flexible and move from being stuck in a present gratification time perspective toward an effective future-oriented time perspective. This is not about genetics. It's about being in a learning environment and culture.

So What?

Viktor Frankl, a Holocaust survivor and author, once wrote that, "[b]etween stimulus and response there is a space. In that space is our power to choose our response. In our response lies our growth and our freedom."

Time perspective is the unique psychological phenomenon that makes us aware of both the space and time to choose a particular response, to which Frankl refers. Although language offers three time perspectives, psychology offers six. These psychological time perspectives are highly influenced by experience, environment, and culture. It is in our best interest, and the interest of our organizations, to not only understand these time perspectives, but to be able to flex between them as circumstances demand. We can create environments and organizational cultures that influence our own time perspectives, the time perspectives of those around us – and, ultimately, the behaviors we see in ourselves and in others.

Next Steps

1. What is your primary time perspective?
2. What is the primary time perspective in your company?

3. Are you getting the creativity and innovation you want and need in your company?

4. If you were going to flex from your current time perspective, which time perspective would you hope to develop and flex towards?

CHAPTER 9

QUINTESSENCE AND CULTURE SHIFT

"I must be willing to give up what I am in
order to become what I will be."

– Albert Einstein,
Physicist

What You Need To Know:

1. Only 5% of the universe is made up of ordinary matter; 95% of the universe is made up of dark matter and dark energy, which are matter and energy that science cannot describe or measure (yet), but knows is there.

2. Quintessence is the "secret sauce" in organizations that have it, and it is comprised of a balance of connectedness, trust, language, and time perspective. Quintessence helps organizations not just survive, but truly thrive, especially in the face of adversity.

3. People don't fear change; people fear loss.

4. There are five steps to creating a shift in culture.

5. Radical change is temporary; permanent change happens incrementally.

Quintessence is not a word that is often heard in modern English. However, in most ancient philosophies (particularly Greek, Hindu, Buddhist, and Japanese traditions), quintessence was the fifth element that existed in addition to the four classical elements (fire, air, water, and earth). The first four elements are considered inert, and it was believed that it was the fifth element, quintessence, that was necessary to bring these elements together to create life. All living creatures were believed to contain different proportions of all five elements.

> Only 5% of the universe is made up of ordinary matter; 95% of the universe is made up of dark matter and dark energy, which are matter and energy that science cannot describe or measure (yet), but knows is there.

In modern physical cosmology and astronomy, quintessence is a form of dark energy. Dark energy is a hypothetical form of energy that permeates all of space and is said to accelerate the expansion of the universe. Dark energy is the most accepted hypothesis to explain observations beginning in the 1990s that indicate that the universe continues to expand at an accelerating rate. According to the Planck mission team, the European Space Agency's mission to observe the first light in the universe, and based on the standard model of cosmology, the total mass–energy of the universe contains 4.9% ordinary matter (what we can see), 26.8% dark matter, and 68.3% dark energy.[1] There are two types of dark energy: (1) a cosmological constant, having a constant density filling space homogenously, and (2) quintessence, which is dynamic, so it can vary in time and space.

As it relates to business, quintessence is what I define as the human energy that is created when the four elements discussed in this book (connectedness, trust, language, and time perspective) are brought into balance to create a strong, effective culture. Quintessence is the element that gives life to a group, business, or organization. It is the element that creates expansion of an organization. It creates the type of commitment and dedication that fuels growth and discretionary effort. It is the element that draws in both customers and employees, in a way that makes it impossible for them to imagine that they could do business or work with anyone else. It is the element that cannot be copied, borrowed, bought, or stolen. It is the element that your competitors want and need – but cannot see.

 Quintessence is the "secret sauce" in organizations that have it, and it is comprised of a balance of connectedness, trust, language, and time perspective. Quintessence helps organizations not just survive, but truly thrive, especially in the face of adversity.

I am not aware of any business schools that teach quintessence. Both business schools and Wall Street analysts continue to think in terms of traditional quarterly numbers and profit without truly understanding what it is that will drive profit in the coming decades. Currently, quintessence is qualitative. It can be assessed by observing the behaviors of members that are part of a particular culture. It is the cultural factor that will provide a competitive advantage in every industry.

Quintessence is part of a new business paradigm. For the bulk of the last century, business objectives involved promoting and selling a company's products, regardless of the real needs of consumers. Businesses, with their large marketing and sales departments, were like predators; consumers and their wallets were their prey. Quintessence is the force that will break this paradigm. It will touch all stakeholders, customers, employees, suppliers, partners, shareholders, and the community, in a way that will ensure mutual benefits for everyone involved in the sales process.

A strong culture powered by quintessence transforms the behaviors of anyone who experiences it; quintessence is the cultural secret ingredient among companies that succeed today and into the future. Members of the culture feel excitement about their companies and infuse that excitement into others, both at work and outside of work. They talk about their company with pride, as if it were their own, and that pride and excitement is passed to current and potential customers. This type of contagion cannot always be seen by people who look exclusively at the numbers in the short-term, but it is most certainly captured in long-term profits.

Quintessence Personified: The Power of Vistage International "Chairs"

Vistage International is the largest CEO and business owner peer-advisory group organization on the planet. Today, it has more than 18,000 members in 16 countries who outperform their competitors and grow at three times the rate than they did before joining Vistage International. It started much smaller.

Robert Nourse founded Vistage International (originally known as The Executive Committee, or "TEC") in 1957 in Milwaukee, Wisconsin. Nourse brought together a group of non-competing executives who met monthly to improve their business performance. The group began with the purpose of discussing business issues they had in common and ways to overcome those challenges. The group members soon found themselves building unique connections with each other and sharing ideas and experiences (related to both business and personal situations) that could help each of them improve their businesses and their lives.

As the organization grew and continued to evolve, they added guest speakers as an educational component for their meetings. The speakers were selected based on their expertise in subjects that could assist the group in its ongoing development, and I've had the pleasure of speaking with Vistage International groups around the world since 2010.

When it reached a critical mass, the organization created a headquarters and invested in the next level of support and guidance: the professional "Chair" (short for "Chairperson"). The role of the Chair would be to facilitate the group meetings and serve as a professional coach to each member.

In 2006, TEC rebranded itself as Vistage International. The name Vistage comes from combining the word "vista" (implying the taking of a "long view") and "advantage" (signifying the competitive advantage that comes from being a member of a CEO peer group).

Vistage International has grown successfully throughout the years because of the experience it provides its members. As with any organization, the success of the whole depends on the contributions of the individuals within each role. It is not a perfect organization; there is no such thing. But it has real strengths in its model, one of which is allowing its Chairs and its members to create a different culture in each group. In my experience as a speaker for Vistage, the most critical influence on the culture of the group – and the type of experience a member will have in that group – is the professional Chair who leads the group.

The fundamental role of a Chair is to create a healthy, productive, and self-sustaining culture for the group. This is in no way an easy task. It has often been said that being a Chair of a group of CEOs is "like herding cats." It is difficult because all the members are very independent and have strong wills of their own. It has also been said that "a group is a reflection of its Chair." This means that the culture (and, ultimately, the success) of the group is a direct result of how the Chair operates in that group.

Vistage International Chairs come from enormously diverse backgrounds with enormously diverse experiences. As you can imagine, each Chair has his or her own distinct personality. Just as no two Chairs are alike, no two groups are alike. The company has yet to identify a single factor (or group of factors) that can predict or ensure the success of a Chair. In my experience, what I have found to be most predictive of a Chair's (and, ultimately, a group's) success is his or her ability to create a culture with quintessence.

In a group, quintessence is created by applying the four cultural factors that have been discussed in this book: connectedness, trust, language, and time perspective. Chairs who are able to apply these concepts are rewarded with a successful group: one that develops quintessence. Not all Vistage International groups have quintessence, but those that do have it offer their members, Chair, and speakers an exceptional experience.

Connectedness and Quintessence

One of my favorite Vistage International Chairs is based in the Midwest. He has been a Chair for many years, and he has a member who has been part of his group for approximately fifteen years, but the member's longevity is not the exceptional part of this story. What is exceptional is that four years ago, the member moved his business from Chicago to Denver, but he continues to meet with his Vistage International group monthly, which remains in Chicago. This means that as a CEO, he is taking 1.5 days (including travel time) a month to continue his connection to his Vistage International group and to his Chair. This is not easy. This is not convenient. This is not inexpensive. But this is what happens when a group has real connectedness embedded in its culture. Connectedness, the sense of real belonging, is the glue of human relationships.

As an outsider, this type of connectedness in the culture of a group can be spotted thirty seconds after you walk into the room and observe how members greet one another. When connectedness and belonging are embedded into a culture, the members don't shake hands – they hug. Now, I can already hear many of you saying, "I'm an introvert, I don't like 'other people' or 'strangers' hugging me." Fair enough. But first, consider that introversion is a personality characteristic that, like most personality characteristics, displays itself differently based on the culture in which it finds itself. Second, if you are a member of a group with this type of culture, these are not "strangers" or "other people"; they are members of a group to which you belong. Even introverted people hug people with whom they feel connected. Finally, as I often tell CEOs, "You can cultivate a culture that is a reflection of your own personality quirks and preferences or you can cultivate a culture that will ensure the longevity of your organization. These are usually mutually exclusive. Choose one." This holds true for the connectedness of Vistage Chairs, groups, and your organization as well.

Observing communication among members also provides immediate clues regarding the group's connectedness (or lack thereof). In most Vistage International groups, it is likely that the members of the group have not seen each other in about a month. When connectedness is a part of the culture, the first communication will be about some personal topic that was discussed in the last meeting. "How did your wife's surgery go?" "How is your son adapting to his new college?" "How did your daughter's soccer game turn out?" Yes, this is a CEO peer group coming together to focus on business, but when connectedness is part of the culture, it is the personal issues that serve as the connective tissue for the group.

When a Chair is able to not only "make it okay" to share personal information in the group, but actually make it part of the fabric of the group's culture, real connection follows. With real connectedness, the culture becomes self-sustaining and you find fertile ground for quintessence to grow and flourish.

Trust and Quintessence

Recall the formula for building trust: trust in a culture develops when its members display reliability, openness, competence, and concern (ROCC). Only then will members of a culture be willing to take risks and be vulnerable.

Most full-day Vistage International meetings are divided into two half-day segments. One half-day segment is for education, where members will normally hear a speaker present on a topic; the other half-day segment is an executive session, where members process issues or discuss the details of what is going right and wrong in their businesses. It is during the executive session portion of the meeting when members have the opportunity to offer feedback to each other. It is particularly during this latter half of the day that trust is paramount to the functioning of a group, not only for the processing of business issues, but for addressing personal issues that arise as well.

As a speaker, it is unusual to take part in the executive session portion of a Vistage International meeting. Upon occasion, in part because I am trained as a psychologist, I have been invited to do so.

On one such occasion, I had presented to a group on the East Coast. A member who had been part of the group for only a few months had a personal issue that needed to be processed. Because he was a relatively new member, he started with some trepidation. The member revealed that he had an aggressive form of cancer. The doctors had given him only about a 20% chance of survival, and said that if he was going to be treated, he would need to go to the Mayo Clinic in Rochester, Minnesota. The treatment would be aggressive, and it would take him from his home and his business for at least six months. His intention was to get some ideas from the group regarding what some of his options might be, including the possibility of trying to get one of his competitors to buy his business.

The group's response was memorable in many ways, and the solution they proposed – and ultimately implemented – illustrated not only trust but also quintessence. First, the group displayed real connection through (1) emotional channels, displaying real emotions such as shock, grief, and even tearful concern; (2) physical channels, with displays of physical affection and comfort, to include hugging and placing their arms around him; and (3) cognitive channels, when some of the members shared their personal stories with cancer and some of the thoughts and fears that they, themselves, had faced and overcome. He learned, in no uncertain terms, that he was connected to them and they were connected to him.

What happened next was even more remarkable. The group decided that they would form what they called a "Tiger Team." This was a group that would take responsibility for his business during this period of crisis. They decided, with his trust and assent, that as a group they would collectively run his business, each individual member taking on a specific role. Some of the group members even volunteered to share the responsibility of the day-to-day operations of the business.

Let me be clear: these were CEOs *who already had their own businesses to run.* They each faced challenges of their own, from personnel issues to financial challenges. These issues were real and, for many of them, pressing. Additionally, even in the best circumstances, I don't know many CEOs who have the time or the inclination to take responsibility for the day-to-day operations of a business that is not their own, particularly if there is no personal financial gain involved for them. Nevertheless, this group proposed sharing CEO and operations duties while the ill member was undergoing treatment.

The cancer treatment took one year (six months longer than anticipated), after which the member returned to the group. During his absence, the Vistage International group members kept him informed, consulted with him regarding any changes that they thought needed to be made, and continued to grow the company.

This is an example of what quintessence provides. These were members of a Vistage International group, with a strong culture that dictated, "You are not alone. We make personal and professional sacrifices for other members of our group, particularly in times of need." They were committed to the group, to each other, and to the culture. It was beautiful to simply be in the room as an observer and watch this unfold.

This example demonstrates how the four factors that lead to trust (reliability, openness, competence, and concern) can shape a group's culture and behaviors – and also how they can evolve into true quintessence. When members of a group meet routinely, develop a culture for that group, and do what they say they are going to do, you have reliability. When members of a group can share the scariest and most difficult events in their lives, you have openness. When members of a group show skill in solving problems – their own and others' – you have competence. When members of a group show genuine affection and demonstrate interest in issues large and small, you have concern. When trust truly becomes part of the fabric of a culture, it grows and nurtures quintessence.

Language and Quintessence

Language as part of a culture can also be observed in routine communication. Cultural language develops as a shorthand for the group to understand complex concepts. This linguistic shorthand can often be seen in the setting of "ground rules" for meetings. For example, some Vistage International groups will use the following rules:

The Big Ben Rule. Everyone's time is valuable. Because coming in late is disruptive, when members show up late, either at the beginning of a meeting or after a break, it diminishes the value of other members' time and the culture of timeliness and respect.

The Disneyland Rule. Disneyland claims to be "the happiest place on earth." Even though the topics discussed in meetings are serious and laden with gravitas, members should still have fun and enjoy the meeting and their lives.

The Aretha Franklin Rule. Aretha Franklin is most known for her song, "Respect." It is a reminder to show respect for members and guests, even when their views may be quite different from your own.

The Vegas Rule. Las Vegas has a motto that "what happens in Vegas, stays in Vegas." Confidentiality in these groups is paramount. What is said in the room, stays in the room.

The T-Rex Rule. The Tyrannosaurus Rex became extinct because it could not adapt to its changing environment. It is a reminder to members that the world is an ever-changing environment. Every member in the room is there to learn, grow, and change. If they are unwilling to do so, they and/or their businesses will share the same fate as the T-Rex.

During the feedback and issues-processing part of the Vistage International meeting day, a shared common language is a key component in understanding the feedback offered.

Another one of my favorite Chairs shared the following story with me. When he was a relatively new Chair with less than five years of experience, he inherited a group that had been together as a group for more than twelve years. He inherited an established group because the previous Chair had retired. It stands to reason that if a group has a core set of members that have been together that long, it has a strong and well-developed culture.

In one of his first meetings as the Chair of this group, during the afternoon period of issue processing, a couple of the group members began to give some feedback to another group member in a way that this Chair, who was new to the group, considered to be "harsh." The Chair, having been a CEO himself when he ran a company, saw an opportunity to intervene to ensure communication was occurring in a way that he thought proper. He began, very appropriately, with, "Excuse me," but before he could continue, one of the group's senior members said to him, "Wait, listen, and learn."

Some might consider this type of language to be condescending. Some might consider it rude. It was neither. The language in the culture of this group was simply direct and meaningful. This was a new Chair in a group that had already been together twelve years. The culture was well-established. Fortunately, he had the wisdom to understand that he was still learning about their language and behavioral norms. He also had the courage and strength to not take the member's response personally and to truly learn from the experience.

One of the lessons was that culture, like that situation, was not about him. It was about the group and its members. Even if he did not like the particular language or intensity with which the feedback was being given, this group by all measures was a successful group. It had a core group of members who had been together for more than twelve years. They had well-established cultural norms for the group and the feedback process.

This is what happens in any strong culture, when a new person who is not familiar with the culture comes in and tries to gently (or sometimes not so gently) correct or redirect behavior. In this case, it was a member correcting the new Chair because the Chair was trying to guide or limit the language and intensity that was being used. For that group at that moment, the language and intensity was within the cultural norm and not a problem. The problem was the Chair trying to intervene when no intervention was necessary, and the culture corrected him for doing so.

When groups in a culture share a common language, it supports connectedness because they are synchronized with one another. It supports trust because they understand each other more precisely with fewer words and less effort. It supports quintessence because members will move mountains to protect, support, and help each other.

Time Perspective and Quintessence

Most successful CEOs tend to be future-goal-oriented people. They are very good at setting a goal, weighing pros and cons, looking at a variety of possibilities, evaluating alternatives, and choosing the best one to get to their desired goal.

Part of the challenge arises from the fact that although profit comes from a future-goal-oriented time perspective (looking towards the future to see how profits can be realized), many CEOs attempt to impose a present-gratification time frame on it ("I want more profit, and I want it now!"). Many CEOs are good at figuring out problems looking towards the future, yet they want profit (or more of it) more immediately and impatiently.

Another part of the time perspective challenge is that human relationships occur in the present. Many CEOs look at interpersonal issues as something they will solve tomorrow or the next day, as if they can apply their future goal orientation to a relationship issue occurring now, in the present. So, using broad brushstrokes, many CEOs want more profit today, while waiting to deal with relationship issues tomorrow.

I'd like to contrast this typical approach with the approach of another one of my favorite Chairs, who has been a successful businessman in his own right for a long time, in part because he has been able to effectively apply the concept of time perspective in his own business. As a Vistage International Chair, he now also helps his members understand and apply time perspective, both in their own businesses and in his Vistage International group.

This Chair corrects the typical CEO time perspective issue by building a culture in the group that focuses on relationships *now* and profit *in the future*. This does not mean that this group does not look at and consider financial statements, because they certainly do. They use a trailing twelve-month profit and loss statement as a metric on a monthly basis, but these financial statements are used primarily as an indicator of efficient and effective performance, and only then as a measure of profit.

This means that a huge part of the group's focus is on the specific relationships that need to change – in the present – to increase performance. The discussion does not consist only of relationships between people, such as between employees or between employees and management, although that is clearly part of the discussion. On a macro level, "relationships in the present" also refers to the relationships between the business and suppliers, the business and customers, and the business and its purpose and cause. On a more micro level, relationships in the present refers to the relationships between an employee and that employee's specific skill set. Is it current? Does it need to be improved or updated? It also refers to the relationship between an employee and the metrics and/or feedback being given. Is it meaningful? Is it actionable? Is it timely?

Relationships go beyond relationships between human beings. We all have relationships with different things in our environment and culture. Each one of these relationships requires an action, from moment to moment, whether we like it or not. The actions taken (or not taken) by employees are the medium in which profit is created. This is where efficiency for future profit happens. This is how relationships need to be addressed in the present time frame.

Profit comes from focusing on the present time frame in order to achieve efficiencies and effectiveness that lead to profit in the future. In certain organizations, a bad month or a bad quarter makes people anxious that "heads will roll." By contrast, in this Vistage group, in this culture, financial metrics are feedback about performance that needs to change – in the present – in order to achieve greater profit in the future. This is how this Chair creates a culture with a time perspective that all members adopt and apply in their own businesses. Present time perspective is applied to relationships. Future time perspective is applied to profit. When these time perspectives are applied in this way, quintessence has an opportunity to flourish.

Cultural Markers of Quintessence

Rather than having to "play by the rules" of conventional marketing practices (and expenses), companies with quintessence experience explosive growth through the powerful connections with their stakeholders that are created as a result of their quintessence. As has long been true, word of mouth becomes a strong marketing tool. Word of mouth is a way to leverage the connectedness component of quintessence.

Companies with quintessence decentralize decision-making in a way that increases top executive *influence* (rather than control) at all levels of the company. This demonstrates trust from executives to employees, creates engagement and ownership, and feeds quintessence.

Companies with quintessence have a cultural value and practice of transparency, and, as a result, have to devote fewer resources to litigation. This is how they leverage openness and trust. When you are open and trustworthy, far fewer adversarial relationships are created, and litigation becomes less necessary to resolve disagreements.

Companies with quintessence develop a cultural language all their own. Its purpose is to communicate complex ideas and actions with fewer words and more efficient expressions. Its effect is greater efficacy and connectedness. Sharing a language increases understanding, ties people together, and supports quintessence.

Publicly traded companies with quintessence do not allow themselves to be controlled by Wall Street expectations. They do not sacrifice long-term growth for short-term quarterly earnings reports, and, in the long run, they have higher price/earnings ratios. Similarly, privately held companies with quintessence maintain that profit comes from a long-term perspective or future goal orientation.

Quintessence in Society

Companies with quintessence show connectedness with others and see their role as positively influencing society, their ultimate stakeholders, rather than just increasing profit and shareholder wealth. They do this in several ways.

1. *They change the competitive context.* Whole Foods Markets shares information in ways that allow all its stakeholders to look at the organization as a collaborative entity. Stakeholders see their own success as tied to the success of Whole Foods Markets and develop an "ownership" mentality.
2. *They set and adhere to standards for the global good.* IKEA uses high environmental, safety, and sustainability standards, even when local regulations don't require them.
3. *They rapidly become part of the local community by responding to local needs.* When Progressive Insurance set up shop in Baltimore, they began by offering jobs to Zurich Insurance Group employees who had recently been laid off.
4. *They cooperate with other organizations and governments.* The state and local governments of California, Virginia, and Texas work with private sector companies to build and maintain infrastructure (roadways, train and metro stations, and so on) with limited impact on taxes. NASA partnered with SpaceX to deliver supplies to the International Space Station.

5. *They encourage and reward employees for volunteering their own time and skills in support of local communities.* Patagonia has an internship program that offers employees two months a year of paid leave to volunteer with an environmental organization that the employee chooses.

Getting from Where You Are to Where You Want to Be

Many people struggle to believe that a social agenda could drive changes in how classic capitalism "typically" works. But the truth is that the trend is already established. Social capitalism proves customers are demanding companies that are more socially aware. Suppliers are demanding to work with companies that create win-win collaborative relationships. Employees are demanding cultures that are sensitive to their lives and the lives they touch.

Many of the companies I discuss in this book already consider society to be their ultimate stakeholder. There are companies today who will continue to focus on short-term profits. These companies will never learn what quintessence is, let alone how to leverage it. By contrast, when a company understands its culture as something that inescapably envelops all its stakeholders, like water does to a fish, then they will see the importance of connectedness, trust, language, time perspective, and quintessence. Companies that are successful in the future will be so because they both have and leverage of quintessence.

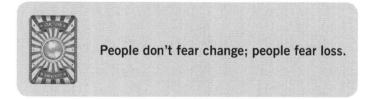

People don't fear change; people fear loss.

Nevertheless, some companies continue to resist change, and they continue to focus on short-term profits while sacrificing long-term success and sustainability. They do so, at least in part, because they believe one or more of the myths that seem to persist about change in general:

Myth 1: Fear and anxiety are powerful motivators for change. In reality, fear produces denial more often than it produces change. In a famous study by Eileen Kelly conducted to understand the drivers of corporate longevity, the majority of companies never saw their 40th anniversary.[2] I would suggest that most (if not all) saw and feared their demise. Yet most continued to do what they'd always done, denying that the environment had changed. When the environment changes, we (and our organizations) must change with it. If we do not, we will perish.

Myth 2: Providing sufficient objective information is enough to change behavior. If this were true, the United States population wouldn't have overweight and obesity rates that hover around 60%, nor would it have more than 43 million smokers. Information alone is not enough to drive behavior change.

Myth 3: People resist and fear change. People don't resist and fear change. People resist and fear *loss*. If you go to an employee who makes $50K a year and tell this person that his or her new salary is $100K a year, that's a change most people will not resist. If you have people around you resisting change, you must address fear of loss. When a culture develops quintessence, through its leveraging of connectedness, trust, language and time perspective, fear is diminished and change happens.

Creating a Shift and Cultural Momentum

Momentum is a term borrowed from physics, specifically Newton's First Law of Motion: "an object in motion will stay in motion unless acted upon by an outside force." Similarly, the concept of "cultural momentum" can be thought of as: "behaviors that are in motion (or part of a routine) will stay in motion (or part of that routine) unless acted upon by an outside force." In order to create a change in our current organizational culture, we must be aware of its current momentum (direction, strength, behaviors) and then follow certain steps to shift that momentum. There are five key steps to creating a shift in cultural momentum, each of which is discussed in detail below.

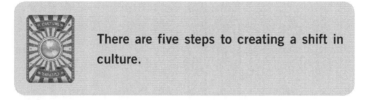

There are five steps to creating a shift in culture.

Step 1: Recognize and honor the strengths of your existing culture.

When assessing culture (or anything else), it is always tempting to "lead with the negative." What is broken? What needs to be fixed? What are the most pressing problems? But bear in mind that whether you love or hate your organization's culture, it is likely a product of good intentions that evolved in unanticipated ways. Most organizations can recognize a cultural value that served the organization originally, but that is currently applied in a way that is harmful.

For example, your organization may have been founded with a strong focus on customer service, and this might still be a core value. However, if an employee believes or is taught that customer service involves a certain fixed cost to the company, that employee might offer resistance to any cost-cutting measures, believing the company would be sacrificing customer service.

Another example might be in the manufacturing sector, where processes and procedures are defined by SOPs (Standard Operating Procedures) that define the model of efficiency for a particular process. Deviation from those processes is typically seen as wasteful and inefficient. Someone who holds strongly to this cultural norm will resist creativity and innovation, as it requires stepping outside of established procedures.

The key to successfully executing Step 1 is to first iden' cuss with current employees the importance of the cultu⸴ underlies one or more behaviors that may have become Emphasize that the underlying *value* is not changing; i *expression* of that value that will change (this will address, in part, the issue of fear of loss discussed earlier). Then, discuss the *new* behaviors that will be associated with the same core value or cause. Remember this key truth about habit change: if we keep the same cue and the same reward, all we need to do is change the routine. Changing the behaviors (creating a cultural shift) is changing the routine. This is much more successful when we keep the same cue and same reward.

Taking Step 1 in a collaborative way will give employees buy-in and make any changes feel less top-down and more like a joint effort that employees can own and embrace. People will protect, defend, and help grow that which they feel is their own. Giving employees ownership of the change ensures they will protect and help grow the new culture. Keep in mind that most companies have groups of employees who are happy to help with a cultural change. These employees can serve as your behavior-change champions and help to maintain important cultural values.

Step 2: Align your culture with your strategy.

Too often, executives try to impose a new strategy from "on high," and, as a result, they experience a great deal of resistance from employees. These same executives will often underestimate the power of culture to support or undermine a strategy. In essence, they forget that culture trumps everything.

One way to avoid this type of error is to begin by asking a vital question: Why do we want or need to change our culture? This is the question that will help executives make the connection between the organization's strategy and any cultural shift they may intend to make. This connection can often come from discussions with employees, and it will further inform any communication initiative that will accompany the new strategy and culture.

Also, rather than coming up with a seemingly endless laundry list of cultural values and behaviors, be focused. One example of a company with a focused set of values is the Mayo Clinic, headquartered in Rochester, Minnesota. They have defined cultural behaviors (norms) that align perfectly with their cause and strategy.

- *Cause:* Diagnose and effectively treat the most complex diseases.
- *Strategy:* Bring together the top specialists across a wide range of medical fields.
- *Cultural norms:* Collaborate and leverage teamwork.

When you align your cultural behavior norms with your cause and strategy, achieving both comes with much less resistance to change.

Step 3: Focus on a few critical behaviors.

You can't ask someone who is completely physically unconditioned to go run a marathon tomorrow. The person must first run 100 feet, then 100 yards, then 300 yards, gradually increasing their distance until they are within striking distance of a marathon. This occurs incrementally, over time.

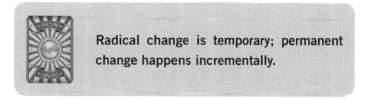

Radical change is temporary; permanent change happens incrementally.

We also see the effects of radical change in behaviors when we see people trying to drop weight precipitously. They may do so temporarily, but in the vast majority of radical weight loss schemes, the weight comes back. This is largely because it takes time to change habit patterns. When people try to change behaviors radically, there is almost always a return to old behavior (habit patterns) because new behaviors (habit patterns) have not been well-established

In Step 1, you observe and identify which values in your culture you would like to keep – plus the associated behaviors that arise from those values, for good or for ill. In Step 3, you want to collect a representative group of leaders across your organization and ask them: If we could create the type of culture we want to have, that would be aligned with the strategy we have chosen, what kind of behaviors would we all have and see in common? Which current behaviors would disappear?

For example, if your company were trying to create a shift in customer service, your leadership teams would ask questions like:

- How should employees treat customers differently?
- What new behaviors would be visible to employees?
- How might employees evaluate each other?
- How could they bring issues up to one another?
- How would employees react to each other's changes in behavior?

When having these discussions, it is important to create a safe environment where these conversations can take place, without fear of alienation or retribution. They should involve thoughtful people throughout the organization and focus on learning what behaviors most affect the current culture, for good and for ill.

Finally, remember that the focal behaviors can be small, as long as they are likely to be emulated and widely recognized throughout the organization. As an example, think back to the story of Paul O'Neill and Alcoa in Chapter 4, Habit Patterns. It was O'Neill's focus on safety that changed the entire system of operations inside Alcoa.

Step 4: Integrate formal and informal initiatives.

As you initiate a focus on new behaviors that align culture and performance, be sure to include both formal and informal initiatives. Formal initiatives include: rules, metrics, incentives, reporting structures, processes and policies, training, leadership and organizational development programs, performance management, compensation and rewards, and internal communication. Informal initiatives include: behavior modeling, genuine manager-employee relationships, internal cross-organizational networks, ad-hoc gatherings, and enlisting influential leaders and employees who will champion cultural change.

Companies tend to favor formal interventions over more informal ones, likely because the informal variety tends to provide data that is both more emotional and more difficult to quantify. However, informal approaches can offer tremendously valuable "organic" information about "the way things really are" in an organization.

Google is a great example of a company that uses informal information in creative and valuable ways. Google has a campus that is often compared to a university campus. At universities, walkways are planned and paved when the university decides to execute an expansion. At Google, they allow employees to walk through the grass, wearing a path from high use, and then pave over the paths that get the most use.

Regardless of the approach you use (and I suggest both), all initiatives should operate at two levels: (1) emotional, which means reaching for connectedness, belongingness, altruism, and pride; and (2) rational self-interest, which means an attention to money, position, title, and external recognition.

Step 5: Measure and monitor cultural shift.

As with any other business initiative, a cultural shift is important to measure and monitor. This will allow all those involved in the cultural shift to recognize any backsliding (which should be immediately addressed) and any necessary course correction. It will also readily identify real improvements that naturalistically serve to support change and increase cultural momentum in the new direction.

The four most important areas to monitor are:

- *Business performance.* Are key performance indicators improving? Are growth targets being achieved with greater frequency? How are sales affected? Have there been any changes in customer complaints?
- *Critical behaviors.* Are individuals across the organization at all levels modeling the identified critical behaviors?
- *Milestones.* Have new policies been implemented? Are employees reaching agreed-upon goals?
- *Beliefs, feelings, and mindsets.* Do employees believe that this change is permanent? Have you seen a visible change in

their attitudes, habits, and mindsets? These will be the last to change. Some employees at first may believe that this cultural shift initiative is another "flavor of the month," meaning just another initiative that is going to die in a quarter or less. If you have involved employees across the organization, leaders at all levels (both positional and interpersonal), then over time you should see a shift in employees' attitudes, feelings, beliefs, and mindsets.

Keep in mind that you get what you measure. Emphasis on quarterly sales performance can lead to undesirable pressure on important customer relationships. If employee retention is a new measure identified by engagement and job satisfaction, both will be important in the retention of top performers as the new cultural shift begins to occur.

Tracking efforts can easily be used to remind everyone of their collective goals. Some companies may send out five- to ten-question surveys every other week to keep a finger on the pulse of the change and get a sense of what behaviors are (and are not) being exhibited. These surveys can serve as a tool to facilitate further dialogue and as reinforcement of the agreed-upon commitment.

Part of the goal is to ensure that measurement doesn't become overwhelming or cumbersome. It is not necessary to invest in or invent a new system. A few carefully worded and designed questions, using specific behavioral measurements tracked on scorecards, are usually more than sufficient.

So What?

Quintessence is the combination and culmination of connectedness, trust, language, and time perspective that creates a secret sauce for your culture. It is the factor that others need but cannot see, even if you were to walk them through your organization, hiding nothing.

Most leaders look to change almost everything else before they will look at culture. I can't tell you the number of times I've gone into an organization and have been told, "We just did a reorganization." This, to me, is code for a situation where the company wasn't meeting its goals, people weren't performing well, things just weren't going right, or something of this nature … and leadership had no idea what to do. So they reorganized.

Reorganizations, unless there is a clear and compelling reason to do them, are often a bit like moving deck chairs around on the Titanic. They do not serve the ultimate purpose of improved performance. As a general rule, organizational structure is not the limiting factor of an organization's success. Culture is the limiter – or the catalyst.

Creating a coherent culture for all your stakeholders and aligning your culture with your strategy and performance metrics ties together everyone who interacts with your organization. This is what creates quintessence.

If you want to create success in your organization, today and into the future, look at culture first. Understand that whatever change is necessary will happen over time, but when you get the culture right, everything else falls into place. Culture trumps everything.

Taking Action

1. Does your company have quintessence? Would your employees agree with you?
2. What are the factors that you see as organizational strengths in your quintessence?
3. What are the factors you see as organizational challenges to quintessence?
4. If you were going to create a shift in your organizational culture, what cultural norms would you want to keep in your organization?
5. What cultural norms would you want to change?
6. How would those changes be tied to your strategy?
7. What are the few critical behaviors you would want to see change?

8. How would you implement formal and informal initiatives to create change?
9. What metrics would you use to monitor change?
10. What would a successful cultural shift look like?

Final Thoughts

Whether we find ourselves leading an organization, a team, a group, or just ourselves, we are responsible for preparing the soil, planting the seeds, and picking the fruits of the culture we create for ourselves and those around us.

This book has discussed the soil to which we must tend, the seeds we must plant, and the fruits we can pick. Behavioral norms (social norms vs. business norms) are the fertile soil in which we plant our seeds. Social proof and habit patterns are the tools we use to plant the seeds. Connectedness, trust, language, and time perspective are the seeds we plant. Quintessence is the fruit we pick, and also a seed. When quintessence is achieved and celebrated, it serves as an additional seed to grow further quintessence. This is how cultures become self-adapting and self-sustaining.

As discussed in the first chapter, culture is very much like a garden. Left unattended, a garden will grow all sorts of weeds and plants that (1) you have no interest in growing, and (2) will actually choke out the fruits, the vegetables, and the flowers you *do* want to grow. We reap what we sow. Therefore, it is up to each of us to plant, nurture, and fully experience the cultures we want to live in ourselves – and share with others.

This is the difference between working *on* your business vs. working *in* your business. Working *on* your business means working *on* your culture, because … *culture trumps everything*.

REFERENCES

Chapter 1: Culture

1. Charles Darwin, *On the Origin of Species by Means of Natural Selection, or the Preservation of Favored Races in the Struggle for Life* (1859).
2. AA Fidanza and R. Fidanza, "A nutrition study involving a group of pregnant women in Assisi, Italy. Part 1: Anthropometry, dietary intake and nutrition knowledge, practices and attitudes," *International Journal for Vitamin and Nutrition Research* 56 (4) (1986): 373-380.
3. AA Fidanza, MS Simonetti, and LM Cucchia, "A nutrition study involving a group of pregnant women in Assisi, Italy. Part 2: Determination of vitamin nutriture," *International Journal for Vitamin and Nutrition Research* 56 (4) (1986): 381-386.
4. Lars Olov Bygren, Gunnar Kaati, and Sören Edvinsson, "Longevity Determined by Paternal Ancestors' Nutrition during Their Slow Growth Period," *Acta Biotheoretica*, Volume 49, Issue 1 (2001): 53-59.
5. "Epigenetics," National Human Genome Research Institute, accessed April 5, 2014, http://www.genome.gov/27532724.
6. "Health, United States, 2013: With Special Feature on Prescription Drugs," U.S. Department of Health and Human Services, Centers for Disease Control and Prevention, National Center for Health Statistics, accessed May 10, 1014, http://www.cdc.gov/nchs/data/hus/hus13.pdf.

7. Susan Swithers, "Artificial sweeteners produce the counterintuitive effect of inducing metabolic derangements," *Trends in Endocrinology and Metabolism*, Volume 24, Issue 9, (2013): 431–441.

8. Aaron W. Schrey et al., "Epigenetic Variation May Compensate for Decreased Genetic Variation with Introductions: A Case Study Using House Sparrows (Passer domesticus) on Two Continents," *Genetics Research International*, Volume 2012 (2012), accessed Nov. 14, 2013, doi.org/10.1155/2012/979751.

9. "National Association of Colleges and Employers Job Outlook Survey," National Association of Colleges and Employers (2013), accessed June 4, 2013, www.naceweb.org.

10. Meghan Casserly, "The Top Five Personality Traits Employers Want," Forbes Magazine, October 4, 2012, accessed March 7, 2013, http://www.forbes.com/sites/meghancasserly/2012/10/04/top-five-personality-traits-employers-hire-most/.

Chapter 2: Behavioral Norms

1. James Heyman and Dan Ariely, "Effort for Payment: A Tale of Two Markets," *Psychological Science* 15 (2004): 787-793.

2. Kathleen Vohs, Nicole Meade, and Miranda Goode, "The Psychological Consequence of Money," *Science*, Vol. 314, 1154 (2006): 1154-1156, accessed February 10, 2013, doi: 10.1126/science.1132491.

3. Stephan Kossmeier, Dan Ariely, and Anat Bracha, "Doing Good or Doing Well? Image Motivation and Monetary Incentives in Behaving Prosocially," *American Economic Review* 99 (2009): 544-555.

4. Uri Gneezy and Aldo Rustichini, "A Fine is a Price," Journal of *Legal Studies* 29 (2000), accessed October 23, 2013, http://rady.ucsd.edu/faculty/directory/gneezy/pub/docs/fine.pdf.

Chapter 3: Corporate Models

1. Martin Seligman, "What is the 'good life'?," *APA Monitor* 29, no. 10 (1998): 2.

2. Adam Smith, *The Wealth of Nations (1776)*, (New York: Modern Library, 1937), 740.

3. Raj Sisodia, David B. Wolfe, and Jagdish Sheth, *Firms of Endearment: How World Class Companies profit from Passion and Purpose*, (New Delhi: Dorling Kindersely (India) Pvt. Ltd., 2007).

4. "Costco Annual Report, 2013," accessed March 27, 2014, http://phx.corporate-ir.net/phoenix.zhtml?c=83830&p=irol-reportsannual.

5. "Wal-Mart Annual Report, 2013," accessed March 25, 2014, http://c46b2bcc0db5865f5a76-91c2ff8eba65983a1c33d-367b8503d02.r78.cf2.rackcdn.com/88/2d/4fdf67184a359f def07b1c3f4732/2013-annual-report-for-walmart-stores-inc_130221024708579502.pdf.

Chapter 4: Habit Patterns

1. Bas Verplanken and Wendy Wood, "Interventions to break and create consumer habits." *Journal of Public Policy & Marketing* 25, no. 1 (2006): 90-103.

2. Ann M. Graybiel, Toshihiko Aosaki, Alice W. Flaherty, and Minoru Kimura. "The basal ganglia and adaptive motor control." *Science* 265, no. 5180 (1994): 1826-1831.

3. Daniel Kahneman, *Thinking, Fast and Slow* (Farrar, Straus and Giroux: New York, 2011).

4. Thomas A. Stewart, "A New Way to Wake Up a Giant." *Fortune* 122, no. 10 (1990): 90.

5. *Ibid.*

6. *Ibid.*

7. Gregory R. Smith, William C. Herbein, and Robert C. Morris. "Front-end innovation at AlliedSignal and Alcoa," *Research-Technology Management* 42, no. 6 (1999): 15-24.

8. Ann M. Graybiel, "Building action repertoires: memory and learning functions of the basal ganglia," *Current Opinion in Neurobiology* 5, no. 6 (1995): 733-741.

9. Doug Lennick and Fred Kiel, *Moral Intelligence: Enhancing Business Performance and Leadership Success* (Upper Saddle River: Wharton School Publishing, 2008).

Chapter 5: Connectedness

1. Vittorio Gallese and Alvin Goldman, "Mirror neurons and the simulation theory of mind-reading," *Trends in Cognitive Sciences* 2, no. 12 (1998): 493-501.

2. Melanie Killen and Frans BM de Waal, "The evolution and development of morality," in *Natural Conflict Resolution*, ed. Filippo Aureli (Berkeley: University of California Press, 2000), 352-372.

3. Frans BM de Waal and Angeline van Roosmalen. "Reconciliation and consolation among chimpanzees," *Behavioral Ecology and Sociobiology* 5, no. 1 (1979): 55-66.

4. Frans BM de Waal, "Food sharing and reciprocal obligations among chimpanzees," *Journal of Human Evolution* 18, no. 5 (1989): 433-459.

5. Jeremy Rifkin, *The Empathic Civilization: The Race to Global Consciousness in a World in Crisis* (New York: Penguin, 2009).

6. Andrew Nicholson, Juanita M. Whalen, and Penny M. Pexman, "Children's processing of emotion in ironic language," *Frontiers in Psychology* 4 (2013), accessed September 8, 2013, doi:10.3389/fpsyg.2013.00691.

7. E. O. Smith, "Yawning: an evolutionary perspective," *Human Evolution* 14, no. 3 (1999): 191-198.

8. Frans BM de Waal and Pier Francesco Ferrari, "Towards a bottom-up perspective on animal and human cognition," *Trends in Cognitive Sciences* 14, no. 5 (2010): 201-207.

9. Richard Byrne et al., "Do Elephants Show Empathy?," *Journal of Consciousness Studies* 15, no. 10-11 (2008): 204-225, accessed January 8, 2013, https://dspace.stir.ac.uk/bitstream/1893/946/1/2008%20Bates_et_al_JCS.pdf.

10. Frans BM de Waal, "The Antiquity of Empathy," *Science* 336, no. 6083 (2012): 874-876.

11. Michael V. Lombardo, Jennifer L. Barnes, Sally J. Wheelwright, and Simon Baron-Cohen. "Self-Referential Cognition and Empathy in Autism." *PLOS ONE* 2, no. 9 (2007), accessed November 30, 2012, doi:10.1371/journal.pone.0000883.

12. de Waal, "The Antiquity of Empathy," 874-876.

13. Victoria Horner, J. Devyn Carter, Malini Suchak, and Frans BM de Waal, "Spontaneous Prosocial Choice by Chimpanzees," *Proceedings of the National Academy of Sciences* 108, no. 33 (2011): 13847-13851.

14. Sarah F. Brosnan and Frans BM de Waal, "Animal behaviour: Fair refusal by capuchin monkeys," *Nature* 428, no. 6979 (2004): 140.

15. Sarah F. Brosnan and Frans BM De Waal, "Monkeys reject unequal pay," *Nature* 425, no. 6955 (2003): 297-299.

16. Bogdan Wojciszke and Andrea E. Abele, "The primacy of communion over agency and its reversals in evaluations," *European Journal of Social Psychology* 38, no. 7 (2008): 1139-1147.

17. Andrea E. Abele and Bogdan Wojciszke, "Agency and Communion from the Perspective of Self Versus Others," *Journal of Personality and Social Psychology* 93, no. 5 (2007): 751, accessed April 25, 2013, http://badania.net/scl/pdf/abele_wojciszke2007.pdf.

18. Alexander M. Todorov, Ida Gobbini, Karla K. Evans, and James V. Haxby, "Spontaneous retrieval of affective person knowledge in face perception," *Neuropsychologia* 45, no. 1 (2007): 163-173,

accessed December 10, 2012, https://psych.princeton.edu/psychology/research/todorov/pdf/Neuropsychologia.pdf.

19. Alexander Todorov and James S. Uleman, "Spontaneous Trait Inferences Are Bound to Actors' Faces: Evidence from a False Recognition Paradigm," *Journal of Personality and Social Psychology* 83, no. 5 (2002): 1051, accessed June 23, 2013, http://ivizlab.sfu.ca/arya/Papers/Others/Trait%20Inferences%20and%20Actors%20Faces.pdf.

Chapter 6: Trust

1. Nora Noffke, Daniel Christian, David Wacey, and Robert M. Hazen, "Microbially Induced Sedimentary Structures Recording an Ancient Ecosystem in the ca. 3.48 Billion-Year-Old Dresser Formation, Pilbara, Western Australia," *Astrobiology* 13, no. 12 (2013): 1103-1124, accessed February 18, 2014, http://online.liebertpub.com/doi/pdf/10.1089/ast.2013.1030.

2. Manoj K. Bhasin et al., "Relaxation Response Induces Temporal Transcriptome Changes in Energy Metabolism, Insulin Secretion and Inflammatory Pathways," *PLOS ONE* 8, no. 5 (2013), accessed August 22, 2013, doi: 10.1371/journal.pone.0062817.

3. Paul Walker, *An Outline of the History of Game Theory* (Christchurch: Department of Economics, University of Canterbury, 1995).

4. Robert Axelrod, "The Evolution of Strategies in the Iterated Prisoner's Dilemma," in *The Dynamics of Norms*, ed. Christina Bicchieri et al. (Cambridge: Cambridge University Press, 1987): 1-16.

5. Aneil K Mishra, "Organizational Responses to Crisis: The Centrality of Trust," in *Trust in Organizations: Frontiers of Theory and Research*, ed. Roderick M. Kramer and Tom R. Tyler (Thousand Oaks; Sage Publications, 1996): 261-87.

6. Kimberly D. Elsbach, Ileana Stigliani, and Amy Stroud, "The Building of Employee Distrust: A Case Study of Hewlett-Packard from 1995 to 2010," *Organizational Dynamics* 41, no. 3 (2012): 254-263, accessed October 17, 2013, http://gsm.ucdavis.edu/sites/main/files/file-attachments/hpcasestudyorg-dynamicsfinal3.pdf.
7. *Ibid.*
8. *Ibid.*
9. *Ibid.*
10. *Ibid.*
11. *Ibid.*
12. *Ibid.*
13. *Ibid.*
14. *Ibid.*
15. *Ibid.*

Chapter 7: Language

1. Dan Isaac Slobin, "Crosslinguistic evidence for the Language-Making Capacity," in *The Crosslinguistic Study of Language Acquisition, Volume 2: Theoretical Issues*, ed. Dan Isaac Slobin (Hillsdale: Lawrence Erlbaum Associates, 1985), 1157-1260.
2. Donald A. DePalma, Benjamin B. Sargent, Thomas Bassetti, and Renato S. Beninatto, *The Price of Translation: A Comprehensive Analysis of Pricing for Globalization Service Buyers* (Lowell: Common Sense Advisory, Inc., 2008), accessed April 4, 2013, http://www.commonsenseadvisory.com/Portals/_default/Knowledgebase/ArticleImages/080428_R_price_of_trans_Preview.pdf.
3. "International Trade Statistics 2011," World Trade Organization, accessed January 5, 2013, http://www.wto.org/english/res_e/statis_e/its2011_e/its11_toc_e.htm.

4. Tim Berners-Lee and Robert Cailliau, "WorldWideWeb: Proposal for a HyperText Project," November 12, 1990, accessed October 28, 2012, http://www.w3.org/Proposal.html.

5. "Internet Live Stats," accessed January 31, 2014, www.internetlivestats.com.

6. E. V. Clark, "Convention and Contrast in Acquiring the Lexicon," in *Cognitive Development and the Development of Word Meaning*, ed. T. B. Seiler and W. Wannenmacher, (Berlin: Springer-Verlag, 1983), 67-89.

7. Eve V. Clark, "The principle of contrast: A constraint on language acquisition," in *Mechanisms of language acquisition*, ed. B. MacWhinney (Hillsdale: Lawrence Erlbaum Associates, 1987), 1-33, accessed February 9, 2013, http://grammar.ucsd.edu/courses/lign270/Clark_1987.pdf.

8. Victor Ginsburgh and Shlomo Weber, *How Many Languages Do We Need?: The Economics of Linguistic Diversity*. (Princeton: Princeton University Press, 2011).

9. Clark, "The principle of contrast: A constraint on language acquisition," 1-33.

Chapter 8: Time Perspective

1. Philip G. Zimbardo and John N. Boyd, "Putting Time in Perspective: A Valid, Reliable Individual-Differences Metric," *Journal of Personality and Social Psychology* 77, no. 6 (1999): 1271-1288, accessed April 5, 2013, http://www.thetimeparadox.com/wp-content/uploads/2012/09/1999PuttingTimeinPerspective.pdf.

2. Walter Mischel, "Processes in delay of gratification," in *Advances in Experimental Social Psychology*, Volume 7, ed. L. Berkowitz (New York: Academic Press, 1974), 249-292.

3. Celeste Kidd, Holly Palmeri, and Richard N. Aslin, "Rational snacking: Young children's decision-making on the marshmal-

low task is moderated by beliefs about environmental reliability," *Cognition* 126, no. 1 (2013): 109-114.

4. Philip Zimbardo and John Boyd, *The Time Paradox: The New Psychology of Time That Will Change Your Life* (New York: Simon and Schuster, 2008).

5. Marc Prensky, "Digital Natives, Digital Immigrants," *On the Horizon*, Vol. 9, no. 5 (2001), accessed December 3, 2012, http://www.marcprensky.com/writing/Prensky%20-%20Digital%20Natives,%20Digital%20Immigrants%20-%20Part1.pdf.

6. K. Anders Ericsson and Neil Charness, "Expert Performance: Its Structure and Acquisition," *American Psychologist* 49, no. 8 (1994): 725-747, accessed November 19, 2012, http://web.mit.edu/6.969/www/readings/expertise.pdf.

7. Prensky, "Digital Natives, Digital Immigrants," 1-6.

8. Elizabeth Dean, "Physical therapy in the 21st century (Part II): Evidence-based practice within the context of evidence-informed practice," *Physiotherapy Theory and Practice* 25, no. 5-6 (2009): 354-368.

9. Britt Wiberg, Marie Wiberg, Maria Grazia Carelli, and Anna Sircova, "A qualitative and quantitative study of seven persons with balanced time perspective (BTP) according to S-ZTPI," in *1st International Conference on Time Perspective and Research: Converging Paths in Psychology Time Theory and Research*, ed. Maria Paula Paixao et al. (ESPACOBRANCO: 2012), 120.

10. Philip G. Zimbardo, Kelli A. Keough, and John N. Boyd, "Present Time Perspective as a Predictor of Risky Driving," *Personality and Individual Differences* 23, no. 6 (1997): 1007-1023, accessed September 27, 2021, http://www.smithbower.com/old/risk_perception/Present%20Time%20Perspective%20as%20a%20Predictor%20of%20Risky%20Driving%3B%20Zimbardo%201997.pdf.

11. Thomas Ashby Wills, James M. Sandy, and Alison M. Yaeger, "Time perspective and early-onset substance use: A model based

on stress–coping theory," *Psychology of Addictive Behaviors* 15, no. 2 (2001): 118.

12. Jens Förster, Ronald S. Friedman, and Nira Liberman, "Temporal Construal Effects on Abstract and Concrete Thinking: Consequences for Insight and Creative Cognition," *Journal of Personality and Social Psychology* 87, no. 2 (2004): 177, accessed June 7, 2013, http://www.socolab.de/content/files/Jens%20pubs/foerster_friedman_liberman2004.pdf.

13. Ilona Boniwell and Philip G. Zimbardo, "Balancing time perspective in pursuit of optimal functioning," in *Positive Psychology in Practice*, ed. P. Alex Linley and Stephen Joseph (Hoboken: Wiley, 2004): 165-178.

14. "Time Perspective Assessments," accessed January 17, 2014, http://www.thetimeparadox.com/surveys

15. Reuben N. Robbins and Angela Bryan, "Relationships Between Future Orientation, Impulsive Sensation Seeking, and Risk Behavior Among Adjudicated Adolescents," *Journal of Adolescent Research* 19, no. 4 (2004): 428-445.

Chapter 9: Quintessence and Culture Shift

1. P. A. R. Ade et al., "Planck 2013 results. I. Overview of products and scientific results," *Astronomy and Astrophysics* no. PlanckMission2013 (2013), accessed July 8, 2013, http://arxiv.org/pdf/1303.5062.pdf.

2. Eileen P. Kelly, "The Living Company: Habits for Survival in a Turbulent Business Environment," *The Academy of Management Executive* 11, no. 3 (1997): 95-97.

ACKNOWLEDGMENTS

There are many people to whom I am grateful for how their lives have been interwoven with mine during the writing of this book.

First and foremost, my wife, Eve. Thank you for your love, your constant encouragement to keep writing (even when I didn't want to!), and your willingness to read through this book (many, many times) and bring your significant English language abilities to bear on my writing. You continue to make my life better in countless ways.

Bob Meceda, my father-in law, whose business acumen always provides a perspective that is reliable and spot-on. Thank you for reading an early draft of this book and applying that acumen to make this book better than it otherwise would have been. Most importantly, thank you for treating me like your own son from the day that we met.

Chip Tafrate. Thank you for your years of friendship and encouragement that writing a book is not only something I *could* do, but something that I *should* do. Your recognition that my perspective on organizations is unique and worthy of sharing was always inspiring.

Ozzie Gontang. Thank you for requesting my culture presentation, even before this book was published. Thank you also for your willingness to read an early version of the book. Most of all, thank you for your friendship. You are a wonderful exemplar of the type of human being we should all strive to be.

Kari Prevost. Thank you for the confidence you had in me to bring me in to meet your leadership team and future leaders at H. G. Fenton. Thank you as well for your eagerness to read of an early version of this book – and for the feedback you provided. I admire you and everyone on the leadership team at H. G. Fenton for your genuine desire to do the right thing. You truly live, eat, and breathe the belief that when you get the culture right, profits follow.

Bob Berry. Thank you for sharing the inner workings and past challenges of your company, DPS Telecom. Thank you also for your early reading of this book and feedback. I am inspired by your curiosity, your desire to learn, and the learning discipline you bring to your life and your company so that everyone around you also benefits.

Gretta Hermes. Thank you for your early reading of the book. Your editing support gave each chapter a shape it previously did not have. Your suggestion for the "call outs" in each chapter was brilliant.

Heather Neil. Your eye for visual design is amazing! Thank you for your cover design and layout. They are better than anything I could have imagined for myself.

Stephanee Killen. Thank you for taking what was previously a mess of a layout and bringing your artful skills to properly layout this book. Your skills and knowledge of layout have made this a better book.

Grace Pierce. Thank you for bringing to bear your years of knowledge in the publication industry to get this book across the finish line to publication. Your time, effort, willingness to work with my crazy schedule, and dedication to this project will always be greatly appreciated.

INDEX

A

Abele, Andrea E. (et al.), 120
Ade, P. A. R. (et al.), 234
Alcoa, 94–97, 220
amygdala, 130, 131
anxiety, 105, 126, 128–134, 138,
    153, 154, 188, 190, 216
Aretha Franklin Rule, The, 209
Ariely, Dan (et al.), 33, 44
Aslin, Richard, 181, 182
Axelrod, Robert, 134, 136

B

basal ganglia, 84–86, 88, 99
behavioral norm, 21, 23–25, 27, 29,
    30, 47, 59, 62, 72, 169, 210, 224
belonging, 34, 64, 65, 70, 83, 89, 92,
    104, 108–110, 112, 119, 121, 205
Benson, Herbert, 132, 133
Berners-Lee, Tim (et al.), 162, 163
Bhasin, Manoj K. (et al.), 230
Big Ben Rule, The, 209
body alarm, vii
Boniwell, Ilona (et al.), 234
Brosnan, Sarah F. (et al.), 118
business norm, 28–36, 38, 40,
    42, 44, 45, 47–51, 71, 224
Bygren, Lars Olov (et al.), 8–10, 14
Byrne, Richard (et al.), 229

C

Cailliau, Robert, 162
cancer, 13, 133, 191, 207, 208

capo, vii, 166
cardiovascular disease, 8, 133
Casserly, Meghan, 226
cause, 25, 28, 31, 34, 37, 39, 40, 42,
    44, 49, 51, 54, 65, 67–71, 74, 76,
    77, 89, 92, 97, 212, 218, 219
CDOs (Collateralized Debt
    Obligations), 191
Centers for Disease Control
    and Prevention, 225
CERN, 162
chaining, 80, 83, 101
Chair, 203–206, 210–213
channel, 115, 116, 207
chimpanzee, 105, 106, 116–118
chunking, 80, 82, 83, 101
Clark, Eve V., 164
classic capitalism, 70, 73, 74, 215
Code of Ethics, 57, 59, 98
collaboration, 28, 33–38, 47,
    121, 126–128, 134, 138, 147,
    150, 152, 153, 166, 167
Collins, Jim, 73
communication, 17, 57, 59, 62, 67, 71,
    108, 109, 119, 120, 132, 137, 149,
    158, 160, 173, 206, 209, 210, 218, 220
Compaq, 144, 148, 150, 153, 154
compassion, xii, 80, 99, 100, 106
competence, 25, 104, 119–121, 123,
    140, 141, 153–155, 206, 208, 209
complex concepts, 158, 160, 173, 209
concern, ix, 28, 43, 49, 50, 56, 65,
    66, 114, 118, 130, 140, 141, 154,
    155, 184, 185, 187, 206–209
connectedness, ix, 25, 34, 83, 89, 92,
    103–110, 112, 113, 115, 116, 118–
    123, 141, 158, 159, 163, 200–202,
    205, 206, 211, 213–216, 221, 222, 224
corporate loyalty, 28, 33, 37
Costco, 72, 75
craving, 80, 88–93, 99
cue, 80, 87–93, 97–99, 101, 218
cultural momentum, 216, 217, 221

customer, 28, 38–40, 54, 57, 65,
    66, 67, 70, 71, 75–77, 95, 142,
    202, 203, 212, 215, 220

D

dark energy, 200, 201
dark matter, 200, 201
Darwin, Charles, 5, 9
de Lavoisier, Antoine-Laurent, 3
de Waal, Frans BM (et al.), 106, 107, 117
Dean, Elizabeth, 233
delay gratification, 176,
    178, 180, 182, 187
DePalma, Donald A. (et al.), 231
Disneyland Rule, The, 209
DNA, 2, 5–7, 9–13, 17, 161
Dow Jones, 73, 74
DPS Telecom, 168, 169, 173, 236
Dresher, Melvin, 134
Dungy, Tony, 93

E

Ellis, Jim, 162
Elsbach, Kimberly D. (et al.), 144
empathy, 100, 106, 109, 112–116
Enron, 55–62, 98
epigenetics, 2, 5, 6, 8, 10–16, 133
epigenome, 6, 10, 13
Ericsson, K. Anders (et al.), 233
experiment, 33–36, 44, 45, 48, 85,
    86, 99, 107, 134, 178–181, 192

F

factors of production, 66
fairness, 106, 117, 118
Fastow, Andrew, 58, 59
fear, 30, 92, 119, 120, 130, 200,
    207, 215, 216, 218, 220
Fidanza, AA. (et al.), 225
fight, flight, or freeze, 130, 132
financial meltdown of 2008,
    178, 191, 192

Fiorina, Carly, 146–154
Firms of Endearment, 70, 72, 74
Flood, Merrill, 134
Folds, Jay, 23, 24
forgiveness, 80, 99, 100, 137
forgiving, 136
Förster, Jens (et al.), 234
fundamental habit pat-
    tern, 94–96, 98, 102
future goal, 183, 187, 188, 191,
    194, 195, 211, 214
future orientation, 176, 179,
    180, 182, 191, 192, 195
future transcendental, 183, 188, 194

G

Gallese, Vittorio (et al.), 228
genetic blueprint, 16
Ginsburgh, Victor (et al.), 232
Global Data Synchronization
    Network, 161
Global Location Number (GLN), 160
GLP1, 15
Gneezy, Uri (et al.), 48
Good to Great, 73, 74
Graybiel, Ann M. (et al.), 98
Grocery Manufacturers of America, 160
GS1, 161, 163

H

habit pattern, 79–84, 86–102,
    134, 219, 220, 224
Happiness Paradox, 54, 63–65
Hewlett, Bill, 142, 147, 150
Hewlett-Packard (HP), 141–154
Heyman, James (et al.), 33
histones, 10–12
holistic expanded present, 188
Hopkins, Claude C., 90, 91
Horner, Victoria (et al.), 229
HP Way, 142–150
Hsieh, Tony, 38, 60–62

HTML (Hyper-Text Markup Language), 162, 163
Human Genome Research Institute, 10
hypertension, 133

I

IBM, 144, 148, 149
Industrial Revolution, 42, 54, 55, 109
inflammatory disease, 133
insulin, 15, 133
integrity, 17, 19, 57, 59, 80, 83, 99, 100, 143, 145, 147, 148, 150, 152
Internet, 109, 118, 144, 162, 163

K

Kahneman, Daniel, 86
Kelly, Eileen P., 216
Kidd, Celeste, 181, 182
Kiel, Fred, 99–101
Killen, Melanie (et al.), 228
Kossmeier, Stephan (et al.), 44

L

language, ix, 25, 129, 130, 157–173, 177, 183, 196, 200–202, 205, 209–211, 213–216, 222, 224
language community, 164, 165
Law of Predictive Behavior, The, xii, 2–4
Lay, Kenneth, 56, 58
Lennick, Doug (et al.), 99–101
limbic brain, 130
Lin, Alfred, 60
Lombardo, Michael V. (et al.), 229

M

made man, 165, 166
Marshmallow Experiment, original, 178–181
updated, 181–183
metabolic derangement, 14
metabolic syndrome, 14, 16

methyl group, 10–13
microorganisms, 126, 127
Minot Air Force Base, 23
mirror neuron, 105, 106, 111, 116
Mischel, Walter, 178–182
Mishra, Aneil K., 140
morality, 106, 107
motivation, 18, 49, 56, 69, 148
MRI, 105, 116
multiple constituencies, 54, 55, 67
Musk, Elon, 38, 67–69

N

NASDAQ, 72–75
National Association of Colleges and Employers Job Outlook Survey, 17, 18
National Center for Health Statistics, 225
National Human Genome Research Institute, 10
neocortex, 105, 130
Nicholson, Andrew (et al.), 113, 114
Noffke, Nora (et al.), 127
Norrbotten, 7–9

O

O'Neill, Paul, 95–97, 220
openness, 118, 132, 140, 141, 153, 155, 206, 208, 209, 213
optimal temporal balance, 193, 194
Overkalix, 8, 9

P

Packard, Dave, 142, 147, 150
Palmeri, Holly, 181, 182
past negative, 183, 184, 194
past positive, 183, 194
PayPal, 38, 67, 68
people work harder for cause than for cash, 28, 34, 37, 44
Pepsodent, 90, 91

PERMA, 64
Platinum Rule of Habit Pattern
    Shift, 80, 91–93, 97
Platt, Lewis E., 144, 146
poverty, 186, 195
Prensky, Marc, 233
present fatalism, 183, 186, 194
present gratification, 183–186,
    191, 194, 196, 211
primary drive, 104, 108,
    110–112, 121, 122
Principle of Contrast, The, 164
Principle of Conventionality, The, 164
Prisoner's Dilemma, The, 134, 135
Profit Paradox, 54, 65
"Prosocial by Choice" study, 117
purpose supersedes pay, 28, 34, 37

Q

quintessence, 199–203, 205–209,
    211, 213–216, 222–224

R

reciprocity, 106, 107, 118, 137, 138
reliability, 127, 140, 141, 143, 152,
    153, 155, 169, 176, 182, 206, 208
reptilian brain, 129, 130
responsibility, xiii, 66, 80, 99,
    100, 143, 171, 187, 208
responsive, 136
reward, 21, 37, 42–44, 47, 50, 54, 66, 70,
    80, 84–93, 97–99, 101, 107, 117, 127,
    144, 179, 182, 186, 191, 215, 218, 220
Rifkin, Jeremy, 109
risk, 8, 14, 30, 37, 39, 50, 68, 90, 92, 96,
    97, 118, 127, 128, 134, 136, 137, 139,
    140, 142, 146, 187, 190, 191, 206
Robbins, Reuben N. (et al.), 195, 196
routine, 80–84, 87–93, 97–99,
    101, 209, 216, 218

S

Sam's Club, 75
Schrey, Aaron W. (et al.), 17
secondary drive, 104, 110–112, 121
secret sauce, 72, 200, 202, 222
Secret Service, 19–21, 23, 24
Seligman, Martin, 63, 64
Serial Shipping Container
    Code (SSCC), 161
shared common language,
    159–171, 173, 210
shareholder, 54, 67, 68, 71, 72,
    75, 77, 149, 150, 202, 214
Sisodia, Raj (et al.), 70
Skilling, Jeffrey, 58, 98
Slobin, Dan Isaac, 231
Smith, Adam, 66
Smith, E. O., 228
Smith, Gregory R. (et al.), 228
social capitalism, 54, 65,
    67, 69–75, 77, 215
social norm, 27–35, 37–45,
    47–51, 71, 151, 224
social proof, 55, 58–63, 76, 77, 83, 224
S&P 500, 73, 74
SpaceX, 38, 68, 214
stakeholder, 54, 67, 70–72, 75–77,
    96, 202, 213–215, 223
Stewart, Thomas A., 227
supply chain, 159–161, 163
Swinmurn, Nick, 60
Swithers, Susan, 14–16
System 1, 87, 88
System 2, 87

T

take money off the table, 34, 41, 121
Tampa Bay Buccaneers, 93
TEC (The Executive
    Committee), 203, 204
time perspective, ix, 25, 165, 175–179,
    181–184, 186–197, 200–202, 205,
    211–213, 215, 216, 222, 224
Time Perspective Assessment, 194

tit-for-tat, 136–138
Todorov, Alexander M. (et al.), 121
T-Rex Rule, The, 209
Truscott, Tom, 162

U

Uniform Product Code (UPC), 160, 161
United States Defense Department's
    Advanced Research Projects
    Agency (DARPA), 162
URL (Uniform Resource Locator), 162
U.S. Department of Health and
    Human Services, 225
Usenet, 162

V

Vegas Rule, The, 209
Venture Frogs, 60
Verplanken, Bas (et al.), 81
Vistage, 203–210, 212, 213
Vohs, Kathleen (et al.), 35
vulnerable, 113, 136, 206

W

Walker, Paul, 230
Wall Street, 76, 149, 151, 202, 214
Wal-Mart, 75
warmth, 104, 118–123
Wealth of Nations, The, 66
Whole Foods, 73, 75, 214 Whole
Trade, 75
Wiberg, Britt (et al.), 233
Wills, Thomas Ashby (et al.), 233
wise guy, vii, 166
Wojciszke, Bogdan (et al.), 120
Wood, Wendy, 81
World Wide Web Consortium
    (W3C), 163

X

X.com, 67, 68

Z

Zappos, 38, 55, 60–63, 110, 127
zero-sum game, 54, 77, 111,
    126, 127, 136, 138
Zimbardo, Philip G. (et al.), 177,
    178, 182–184, 188, 193–195

ABOUT THE AUTHOR

Dr. Gustavo Grodnitzky is a speaker, consultant, psychologist and author whose diverse background brings a unique and multidimensional perspective to his global clients. After obtaining his Ph.D. in clinical and school psychology, he completed post-docs in both cognitive therapy and forensic psychology. He has previously run an inpatient drug rehabilitation unit in a correctional institution and an outpatient mental health center.

For the past 15 years, Dr. Grodnitzky has focused on engagements with corporate clients, and he has worked with Global 1000 companies around the world, as well as with smaller, often family-run, businesses. As a consultant and professional speaker, he has delivered more than 1,000 presentations on a variety of topics, including corporate culture, emotional intelligence, anger management, and integrating multigenerational workforces.

When not traveling to see clients or give presentations, Dr. Grodnitzky lives in the mountains west of Denver, Colorado with his wife and his Black Lab.